Easy Home Cooking

BAKING SECRETS

Easy Home Cooking™

BAKING SECRETS

Memorable Cakes

You'll find fabulous recipes for moist chocolate cake, spicy carrot cake, classic sour cream pound cake and more in this collection of delightful cakes.

White Chocolate Cheesecake

- **½ cup (1 stick) butter or margarine**
- **¾ cup sugar, divided**
- **1½ teaspoon vanilla, divided**
- **1 cup flour**
- **4 packages (8 ounces each) PHILADELPHIA BRAND® Cream Cheese, softened**
- **4 eggs**
- **2 packages (6 ounces each) BAKER'S® Premium White Chocolate Baking Squares, melted, slightly cooled**

MIX butter, ¼ cup of the sugar and ½ teaspoon of the vanilla with electric mixer on medium speed until light and fluffy. Gradually add flour, mixing on low speed until blended. Press onto bottom of 9-inch springform pan; prick with fork. Bake at 325°F for 25 minutes or until edges are light golden brown.

MIX cream cheese, remaining ½ cup sugar and 1 teaspoon vanilla with electric mixer on medium speed until well blended. Add eggs, 1 at a time, mixing on low speed after each addition just until blended. Blend in melted chocolate. Pour over crust.

BAKE at 325°F for 55 minutes to 1 hour or until center is almost set. Run knife or metal spatula around rim of pan to loosen cake; cool before removing rim of pan. Refrigerate 4 hours or overnight. Garnish, if desired. *Makes 12 servings*

Prep time: 35 minutes plus refrigerating
Bake time: 1 hour

White Chocolate Macadamia Nut Cheesecake: Stir 1 jar (3½ ounces) macadamia nuts, chopped (about ¾ cup), into batter.

White Chocolate Cheesecake

Mom's Favorite White Cake

Mom's Favorite White Cake

- 2¼ cups cake flour
- 1 tablespoon baking powder
- ½ teaspoon salt
- 1½ cups sugar
- ½ cup butter or margarine, softened
- 4 egg whites
- 2 teaspoons vanilla
- 1 cup milk
- Strawberry Frosting (recipe follows)
- Fruit Filling (recipe follows)
- Fresh strawberries (optional)

PREHEAT oven to 350°F. Line bottoms of two 9-inch round cake pans with waxed paper; lightly grease paper. Combine flour, baking powder and salt in medium bowl.

BEAT sugar and butter in large bowl with electric mixer at medium speed until light and fluffy. Add egg whites, two at a time, beating well after each addition. Add vanilla; beat until blended. At low speed, add flour mixture alternately with milk, beating well after each addition. Pour batter evenly into prepared pans.

BAKE 25 minutes or until wooden pick inserted into centers comes out clean. Cool layers in pans on wire rack 10 minutes. Loosen edges and invert layers onto racks to cool completely.

PREPARE Strawberry Frosting and Fruit Filling. To fill and frost cake, place one layer on cake plate; spread top with Fruit Filling. Place second layer over filling. Frost top and sides with Strawberry Frosting. Place strawberries on top of cake, if desired. Refrigerate; allow cake to stand at room temperature 15 minutes before serving. *Makes 12 servings*

Strawberry Frosting

2 envelopes (1.3 ounces each) whipped topping mix
⅔ cup milk
1 cup (6 ounces) white chocolate chips, melted
¼ cup strawberry jam

BEAT whipped topping mix and milk in medium bowl with electric mixer on low speed until blended. Beat on high speed 4 minutes until topping thickens and forms peaks. With mixer at low speed, beat melted chocolate into topping. Add jam; beat until blended. Chill 15 minutes or until spreading consistency.

Fruit Filling

1 cup Strawberry Frosting (recipe above)
1 can (8 ounces) crushed pineapple, drained
1 cup sliced strawberries

COMBINE Strawberry Frosting, pineapple and strawberries in medium bowl; mix well.

Spicy Gingerbread

2 cups all-purpose flour
1 cup light molasses
¾ cup buttermilk
½ cup granulated sugar
½ cup FLEISCHMANN'S® 70% Corn Oil Spread, softened
¼ cup EGG BEATERS® Healthy Egg Substitute
2 teaspoons baking soda
1 teaspoon ground cinnamon
½ teaspoon ground ginger
¼ teaspoon ground cloves
Powdered sugar, optional

In large bowl, with electric mixer at low speed, beat flour, molasses, buttermilk, granulated sugar, spread, Egg Beaters, baking soda, cinnamon, ginger and cloves until moistened; scrape side and bottom of bowl. Beat at medium speed for 3 minutes. Spread batter into greased 9-inch square baking pan. Bake at 350°F for 1 hour or until toothpick inserted in center comes out clean. Cool in pan on wire rack. Dust with powdered sugar before serving, if desired. Cut into 16 (2-inch) squares.
Makes 16 servings

Prep time: 20 minutes
Cook time: 1 hour

Philly 3-Step™ Fruit Topped Cheesecake

2 packages (8 ounces each) PHILADELPHIA BRAND® Cream Cheese, softened
½ cup sugar
½ teaspoon vanilla
2 eggs
1 ready-to-use graham cracker pie crust (6 ounces or 9 inches)
2 cups fresh fruit slices
2 tablespoons KRAFT® Strawberry or Apple Jelly, heated (optional)

1. MIX cream cheese, sugar and vanilla with electric mixer on medium speed until well blended. Add eggs; mix until blended.

2. POUR into crust.

3. BAKE at 350°F for 40 minutes or until center is almost set. Cool. Refrigerate 3 hours or overnight. Top with fruit; drizzle with jelly, if desired. *Makes 8 servings*

Prep time: 10 minutes
Bake time: 40 minutes

Sour Cream Pound Cake

- **3 cups sugar**
- **1 cup (2 sticks) butter, softened**
- **1 teaspoon vanilla**
- **1 teaspoon lemon extract**
- **6 eggs**
- **3 cups cake flour**
- **¼ teaspoon baking soda**
- **1 cup dairy sour cream**

Heat oven to 325°F. Butter and flour 10-inch tube pan. In large bowl, beat sugar and butter until light and fluffy. Add vanilla and lemon extract; mix well. Add eggs, one at a time, beating well after each addition. In medium bowl, combine flour and baking soda. Add to butter mixture alternately with sour cream, beating well after each addition. Pour batter into pan. Bake 1 hour and 20 minutes or until toothpick inserted in center comes out clean. Cool in pan 15 minutes; invert onto wire rack and cool completely. Store tightly covered. *Makes 16 to 20 servings*

Favorite recipe from **Southeast United Dairy Industry Association, Inc.**

BAKING SECRET

If cake layers cool too long in baking pans, they will be difficult to remove. If this happens simply place the pans in a preheated 350°F oven for 3 to 5 minutes, then turn the layers out onto wire racks.

Fudge Truffle Cheesecake

- **Chocolate Crumb Crust (recipe follows)**
- **2 cups (12-ounce package) HERSHEY'S® Semi-Sweet Chocolate Chips**
- **3 packages (8 ounces each) cream cheese, softened**
- **1 can (14 ounces) sweetened condensed milk (not evaporated milk)**
- **4 eggs**
- **2 teaspoons vanilla extract**

Prepare Chocolate Crumb Crust. Heat oven to 300°F. In microwave-safe bowl, place chocolate chips. Microwave at HIGH (100%) 1½ minutes; stir. If necessary, microwave at HIGH an additional 15 seconds at a time, stirring after each heating, just until chips are melted when stirred. In large bowl, beat cream cheese until fluffy. Gradually beat in sweetened condensed milk until smooth. Add melted chips, eggs and vanilla; mix well. Pour into prepared crust. Bake 1 hour and 5 minutes or until center is set. Remove from oven to wire rack. With knife, loosen cake from side of pan. Cool completely; remove side of pan. Refrigerate several hours before serving. Garnish as desired. Cover; refrigerate leftover cheesecake.

Makes 10 to 12 servings

Chocolate Crumb Crust: In medium bowl, stir together 1½ cups vanilla wafer crumbs, ½ cup powdered sugar, ⅓ cup HERSHEY'S® Cocoa and ⅓ cup melted butter or margarine. Press firmly onto bottom of 9-inch springform pan.

Sour Cream Pound Cake

Karen Ann's Lemon Cake

2 cups all-purpose flour
1½ teaspoons baking powder
½ teaspoon baking soda
¼ teaspoon salt
⅔ cup butter or margarine, softened
1¼ cups granulated sugar
3 eggs, separated
¾ cup sour cream
Grated peel of 1 SUNKIST® Lemon
Lemony Frosting (recipe follows)

Line two 8-inch round cake pans with waxed paper. Preheat oven to 350°F. In medium bowl, combine flour, baking powder, baking soda and salt. In large bowl, with electric mixer, cream butter and sugar. Beat in egg yolks one at a time; beat until light in color. Add flour mixture alternately with sour cream, beating just until smooth. With clean beaters, beat egg whites until soft peaks form. Fold beaten egg whites and lemon peel into batter. Pour batter into prepared pans. Bake at 350°F for 30 to 35 minutes or until wooden pick inserted in center comes out clean. Cool 10 minutes. Remove from pans and peel off waxed paper. Cool on wire racks. Fill and frost with Lemony Frosting.

Makes 12 servings

Lemony Frosting

½ cup butter or margarine, softened
3 cups confectioners' sugar, divided
Grated peel of ½ SUNKIST® Lemon
2 tablespoons fresh squeezed lemon juice

In medium bowl, cream together butter and 1 cup confectioners' sugar. Add lemon peel, lemon juice and remaining 2 cups sugar; beat until smooth.

Makes about 1¾ cups frosting

Frosted Peanut Butter Cake Squares

About 30 REESE'S® Peanut Butter Cup Miniatures
⅓ cup butter or margarine, softened
½ cup REESE'S® Creamy or Crunchy Peanut Butter
⅓ cup granulated sugar
⅓ cup packed light brown sugar
½ cup milk
2 eggs
1 teaspoon vanilla extract
1 cup all-purpose flour
1 teaspoon baking soda
¼ teaspoon salt
Chocolate Peanut Butter Topping (recipe follows)

Heat oven to 350°F. Remove wrappers from candies. Chop candies into pieces. Grease 13×9×2-inch baking pan. In small mixer bowl, beat butter, peanut butter, granulated sugar and brown sugar until well blended. Gradually add milk, eggs and vanilla, beating until smooth and well blended. Stir together flour, baking soda and salt. Add to butter mixture; beat until well blended. Spread batter into prepared pan. Bake 18 to 20 minutes or until wooden pick inserted in center comes out clean. Cool completely in pan on wire rack. Prepare Chocolate Peanut Butter Topping; spread over cake. Sprinkle candy pieces over top. Cut into squares.

Makes 12 to 14 servings

Chocolate Peanut Butter Topping

½ cup HERSHEY'S® Semi-Sweet Chocolate Chips
⅓ cup REESE'S® Creamy Peanut Butter
2 tablespoons butter or margarine
¼ cup powdered sugar

In medium microwave-safe bowl, place chocolate chips, peanut butter and butter. Microwave at HIGH (100%) 1 minute; stir. If necessary, microwave at HIGH an additional 15 seconds at a time, stirring after each addition, just until chips are melted when stirred. Add powdered sugar; whisk until smooth and of spreading consistency.

BAKING SECRET

For easier frosting and decorating, place cooled cake layers in the freezer for 30 to 45 minutes before frosting.

Chocolate Mayonnaise Cake

2 cups all-purpose flour
⅔ cup unsweetened cocoa
1¼ teaspoons baking soda
¼ teaspoon baking powder
3 eggs
1⅔ cups sugar
1 teaspoon vanilla
1 cup HELLMANN'S® or BEST FOODS® Real or Light Mayonnaise or Low Fat Mayonnaise Dressing
1⅓ cups water

Grease and flour bottoms of two 9×1½-inch round cake pans. In medium bowl, combine flour, cocoa, baking soda and baking powder; set aside. In large bowl with mixer at high speed, beat eggs, sugar and vanilla, scraping bowl occasionally, 3 minutes or until smooth and creamy. Reduce speed to low; beat in mayonnaise until blended. Add flour mixture in 4 additions alternately with water, beginning and ending with flour mixture. Pour into prepared pans. Bake in 350°F oven 30 to 35 minutes or until cake springs back when touched lightly in center. Cool in pans on wire racks 10 minutes. Remove from pans; cool completely on racks. Fill and frost as desired.

Makes 1 (9-inch) layer cake

Spicy Butterscotch Snack Cake

1 cup (2 sticks) butter or margarine, softened
1 cup sugar
2 eggs
½ teaspoon vanilla extract
½ cup applesauce
2½ cups all-purpose flour
1½ to 2 teaspoons ground cinnamon
1 teaspoon baking soda
½ teaspoon salt
1⅔ cups (10-ounce package) HERSHEY'S® Butterscotch Chips
1 cup chopped pecans (optional)
Powdered sugar (optional)

Heat oven to 350°F. Lightly grease 13×9×2-inch baking pan. In large mixer bowl, beat butter and sugar until light and fluffy. Add eggs and vanilla; beat well. Mix in applesauce. Stir together flour, cinnamon, baking soda and salt; gradually add to butter mixture, mixing well. Stir in butterscotch chips and pecans, if desired. Spread into prepared pan. Bake 35 to 40 minutes or until wooden pick inserted in center comes out clean. Cool completely in pan on wire rack. Sprinkle with powdered sugar, if desired.

Makes 12 servings

German Sweet Chocolate Cake

1 package (4 ounces) BAKER'S® GERMAN'S Sweet Chocolate
½ cup water
2 cups all-purpose flour
1 teaspoon baking soda
¼ teaspoon salt
1 cup (2 sticks) butter or margarine, softened
2 cups sugar
4 egg yolks
1 teaspoon vanilla
1 cup buttermilk
4 egg whites
Classic Coconut-Pecan Filling and Frosting (recipe follows)

HEAT oven to 350°F. Line bottoms of 3 (9-inch) round cake pans with waxed paper.

MICROWAVE chocolate and water in large microwavable bowl on HIGH 1½ to 2 minutes or until chocolate is almost melted, stirring halfway through heating time. *Stir until chocolate is completely melted.*

MIX flour, baking soda and salt; set aside. Beat butter and sugar in large bowl with electric mixer on medium speed until light and fluffy. Add egg yolks, 1 at a time, beating well after each addition. Stir in chocolate mixture and vanilla. Add flour mixture alternately with buttermilk, beating after each addition until smooth.

BEAT egg whites in another large bowl with electric mixer on high speed until they form stiff peaks. Gently stir into batter. Pour batter into prepared pans.

BAKE 30 minutes or until cake springs back when lightly touched in center. Immediately run spatula between cakes and sides of pans. Cool in pans 15 minutes. Remove from pans. Peel off waxed paper. Cool completely on wire racks.

SPREAD Classic Coconut-Pecan Filling and Frosting between layers and over top of cake. *Makes 12 servings*

Prep time: 40 minutes
Cook time: 30 minutes

Classic Coconut-Pecan Filling and Frosting

1 can (12 ounces) evaporated milk
1½ cups sugar
¾ cup (1½ sticks) butter or margarine
4 egg yolks, slightly beaten
1½ teaspoons vanilla
1 package (7 ounces) BAKER'S® ANGEL FLAKE® Coconut (about 2⅔ cups)
1½ cups chopped pecans

STIR milk, sugar, butter, egg yolks and vanilla in large saucepan. Cook over medium heat until mixture thickens and is golden brown, about 12 minutes, stirring constantly. Remove from heat.

STIR in coconut and pecans. Cool until room temperature and of spreading consistency. *Makes about 4¼ cups*

Prep time: 20 minutes

From top: German Sweet Chocolate Cake, Wellesley Fudge Cake (page 12)

Wellesley Fudge Cake

- 4 squares BAKER'S® Unsweetened Chocolate
- 1¾ cups sugar, divided
- ½ cup water
- 1⅔ cups all-purpose flour
- 1 teaspoon baking soda
- ¼ teaspoon salt
- ½ cup (1 stick) butter or margarine, softened
- 3 eggs
- ¾ cup milk
- 1 teaspoon vanilla

HEAT oven to 350°F.

MICROWAVE chocolate, ½ cup sugar and water in large microwavable bowl on HIGH 1 to 2 minutes or until chocolate is almost melted, stirring halfway through heating time. Stir until chocolate is completely melted; cool.

MIX flour, baking soda and salt; set aside. Beat butter and remaining 1¼ cups sugar in large bowl with electric mixer on medium speed until light and fluffy. Add eggs, 1 at a time, beating well after each addition. Add flour mixture alternately with milk, beating after each addition until smooth. Stir in chocolate mixture and vanilla. Pour into 2 greased and floured 9-inch round cake pans.

BAKE 30 to 35 minutes or until cake springs back when lightly touched. Cool 10 minutes; remove from pans. Cool on wire racks. Frost as desired.

Makes 12 servings

Prep time: 30 minutes
Cook time: 35 minutes

Carrot Layer Cake

CAKE

- 1 package DUNCAN HINES® Moist Deluxe Yellow Cake Mix
- 4 eggs
- ½ cup CRISCO® Oil or CRISCO® PURITAN® Canola Oil
- 3 cups grated carrots
- 1 cup finely chopped nuts
- 2 teaspoons ground cinnamon

CREAM CHEESE FROSTING

- 1 (8-ounce) package cream cheese, softened
- ¼ cup butter or margarine, softened
- 2 teaspoons vanilla extract
- 4 cups confectioners sugar

1. Preheat oven to 350°F. Grease and flour 2 (8- or 9-inch) round baking pans.

2. For cake, combine cake mix, eggs, oil, carrots, nuts and cinnamon in large bowl. Beat at low speed with electric mixer until moistened. Beat at medium speed for 2 minutes. Pour into pans. Bake at 350°F for 35 to 40 minutes or until toothpick inserted in centers comes out clean. Cool.

3. For frosting, place cream cheese, butter and vanilla extract in large bowl. Beat at low speed until smooth and creamy. Add confectioners sugar gradually, beating until smooth. Add more sugar to thicken, or milk or water to thin frosting, as needed. Fill and frost cooled cake. Garnish with whole pecans.

Makes 12 to 16 servings

Carrot Layer Cake

Irresistible Pies & Tarts

Freshly baked apple pie cooling in the kitchen, rich and gooey pecan pie and spicy pumpkin pie all remind us of happy occasions shared with family and friends. Continue to celebrate the good times with these irresistible pies and tarts.

Fruit Tart

⅓ cup FLEISCHMANN'S® 70% Corn Oil Spread
1¼ cups all-purpose flour
4 to 5 tablespoons ice water
1 cup EGG BEATERS® Healthy Egg Substitute
⅓ cup sugar
1 teaspoon vanilla extract
1¼ cups skim milk, scalded
1 cup sliced fresh fruit

In medium bowl, cut spread into flour until mixture resembles coarse crumbs. Add water, 1 tablespoon at a time, tossing until moistened. Shape into a ball. On floured surface, roll dough into 11-inch circle, about ⅛ inch thick. Place in 9-inch pie plate, making a ½-inch-high fluted edge; set aside.

In medium bowl, combine Egg Beaters, sugar and vanilla; gradually stir in milk. Pour into prepared crust. Bake at 350°F for 45 to 50 minutes or until set. Cool completely on wire rack. Cover; chill until firm, about 2 hours. To serve, top with fruit.

Makes 10 servings

Prep time: 30 minutes
Cook time: 45 minutes

BAKING SECRET

Rolling out a pastry crust is a breeze with a canvas pastry cloth. Simply dust the cloth generously with flour and roll out the dough to the appropriate size. Always wash the cloth after each use.

Fruit Tart

Classic Pecan Pie

- 3 eggs
- 1 cup sugar
- 1 cup KARO® Light or Dark Corn Syrup
- 2 tablespoons MAZOLA® margarine or butter, melted
- 1 teaspoon vanilla
- 1½ cups pecans
- Easy-As-Pie Crust (page 23) or 1 (9-inch) frozen deep dish pie crust*

*To use prepared frozen pie crust: Do not thaw. Preheat oven and a cookie sheet. Pour filling into frozen crust. Bake on cookie sheet.

Preheat oven to 350°F. In medium bowl with fork beat eggs slightly. Add sugar, corn syrup, margarine and vanilla; stir until well blended. Stir in pecans. Pour into pie crust.

Bake 50 to 55 minutes or until knife inserted halfway between center and edge comes out clean. Cool on wire rack.

Makes 8 servings

Prep time: 6 minutes
Bake time: 50 minutes, plus cooling

Almond Amaretto Pie: Substitute 1 cup sliced almonds for pecans. Add 2 tablespoons almond flavored liqueur and ½ teaspoon almond extract to filling.

Butterscotch Pecan Pie: Omit margarine; add ¼ cup heavy or whipping cream to filling.

Chocolate Chip Walnut Pie: Substitute 1 cup walnuts, coarsely chopped, for pecans. Sprinkle ½ cup semisweet chocolate chips over bottom of pie crust. Carefully pour filling into pie crust.

BAKING SECRET

To measure flour accurately, spoon it into a dry measure until the measure is overflowing. Then with a straight-edged metal spatula, sweep across the top of the measure. Do not scoop the flour with the measure or tap the measure on the counter, because this will compact the flour and result in an inaccurate measure.

Country Fruit Pie

- 2 pie crust sticks
- 5 fresh California peaches or nectarines, each cut into 8 slices (about 3 cups)
- 3 fresh California plums, each cut into 6 slices (about 1 cup)
- ⅓ cup honey
- 3 tablespoons all-purpose flour
- ½ teaspoon almond extract

Preheat oven to 400°F. Roll out 1 pie crust stick according to package directions to fit 8-inch pie dish. Roll out remaining pie crust stick; cut out about 35 leaf shapes with small leaf-shaped cutter. Gently toss fruit, honey, flour and almond extract in large bowl. Spoon fruit mixture into crust. Place 8 leaf cut-outs over fruit; press remaining leaves onto rim of pie crust with small amount of water. Bake 25 to 30 minutes or until crust is browned and fruit is easily pierced with knife.

Makes 8 servings

Favorite recipe from **California Tree Fruit Agreement**

From top: Almond Amaretto Pie, Classic Pecan Pie

Hazelnut Plum Tart

- **1 cup hazelnuts**
- **¼ cup firmly packed light brown sugar**
- **1 cup all-purpose flour**
- **⅓ cup FILIPPO BERIO® Olive Oil**
- **1 egg, separated**
- **Pinch salt**
- **3 tablespoons granulated sugar**
- **2 teaspoons cornstarch**
- **½ teaspoon grated lime peel**
- **Pinch ground nutmeg**
- **Pinch ground cloves**
- **1¼ pounds plums (about 5 large), halved and pitted**
- **3 tablespoons currant jelly**
- **Sweetened whipped cream (optional)**

Preheat oven to 375°F. Grease 9-inch tart pan with removable bottom with olive oil.

Place hazelnuts in food processor; process until coarsely chopped. Remove ¼ cup for garnish; set aside. Add brown sugar; process until nuts are finely ground. Add flour, olive oil, egg yolk and salt; process until combined. (Mixture will be crumbly.)

Spoon mixture into prepared pan. Press firmly in even layer on bottom and up side. Brush inside of crust with slightly beaten egg white. Place crust in freezer 10 minutes.

In large bowl, combine granulated sugar, cornstarch, lime peel, nutmeg and cloves. Cut each plum half into 4 wedges. Add to sugar mixture; toss until combined. Arrange plums in overlapping circles in crust; spoon any remaining sugar mixture over plums. Place tart on baking sheet.

Bake 45 to 50 minutes or until fruit is tender and juices are thickened. Cool 30 minutes on wire rack. Place currant jelly in small saucepan; heat over low heat, stirring frequently, until melted. Brush over plums; sprinkle with reserved hazelnuts. Serve tart warm or at room temperature with whipped cream, if desired.

Makes 6 servings

Hazelnut Plum Tart

Chocolate Brandy Pie

PIE SHELL

1¼ cups all-purpose flour
1 tablespoon sugar
½ teaspoon salt
6 tablespoons butter
1 egg
1 to 2 tablespoons water

FILLING

¼ cup all-purpose flour
½ teaspoon baking soda
Pinch salt
¾ cup strong coffee
¼ cup brandy
½ cup butter
2 ounces unsweetened chocolate
1 cup BLUE DIAMOND® Blanched Almond Paste
1 cup sugar
1 egg, beaten
½ teaspoon vanilla extract
½ teaspoon almond extract

GARNISH

Whipped cream
Chocolate shavings

To prepare pie shell in food processor, combine flour, sugar and salt. Add butter and mix with on-off bursts until mixture resembles coarse cornmeal.* *Do not overmix*. Add egg and enough water just to form dough. Shape dough into ball and chill 30 minutes. Roll dough out on lightly floured board. Fit into 9-inch pie pan; chill 30 minutes. Prick bottom of pastry shell with fork. Line with waxed paper and fill with dried beans. Bake at 400°F. for 10 minutes. Remove paper and beans; reserve shell.

To prepare filling, sift flour, baking soda and salt; set aside. In a double boiler, over simmering water, heat coffee and brandy. Add butter and chocolate, stirring until melted and smooth. Remove from heat; set aside. Beat almond paste and sugar until mixture resembles coarse cornmeal. Add egg and extracts, beating until smooth. Blend in flour mixture. Gradually add chocolate mixture, scraping sides of bowl occasionally. Pour into prepared pie shell. Bake at 275°F. for 1½ hours. Cool on wire rack. Garnish with whipped cream and chocolate shavings.

Makes 8 to 10 servings

*To prepare by hand, combine flour, sugar and salt. With fingertips or pastry cutter, work butter into flour mixture until mixture resembles coarse cornmeal.

Praline Pie

1 (9-inch) HONEY MAID® Honey Graham Pie Crust
1 egg white, slightly beaten
¼ cup margarine, melted
1 cup firmly packed light brown sugar
¾ cup all-purpose flour
1 teaspoon baking powder
1 egg
1 teaspoon vanilla extract
1 cup PLANTERS® Pecans, coarsely chopped
Prepared whipped topping, for garnish

Preheat oven to 375°F. Brush pie crust with egg white. Bake at 375°F for 5 minutes; set aside. *Decrease oven temperature to 350°F.*

In medium bowl, with electric mixer at low speed, beat margarine and brown sugar until blended. Mix in flour, baking powder, egg and vanilla until well combined. Stir in ¾ cup pecans. Spread in prepared crust; sprinkle top with remaining ¼ cup pecans. Bake at 350°F for 25 to 30 minutes or until lightly browned and filling is set. Cool completely on wire rack. Garnish with whipped topping. *Makes 6 servings*

Pumpkin Cheese-Swirled Pie

1 package (3 ounces) cream cheese, softened
½ cup KARO® Light Corn Syrup, divided
½ teaspoon vanilla
1 cup canned solid pack pumpkin
2 eggs
½ cup evaporated milk
¼ cup sugar
2 teaspoons pumpkin pie spice
¼ teaspoon salt
Easy-As-Pie Crust (page 23) or 1 (9-inch) frozen deep dish pie crust*

*To use prepared frozen pie crust: Do not thaw. Preheat oven and a cookie sheet. Pour filling into frozen crust. Bake on cookie sheet.

Preheat oven to 325°F. In small bowl with mixer at medium speed, beat cream cheese until light and fluffy. Gradually beat in ¼ cup corn syrup and vanilla until smooth; set aside. In medium bowl combine pumpkin, eggs, evaporated milk, remaining ¼ cup corn syrup, sugar, pumpkin pie spice and salt. Beat until smooth. Pour into pie crust. Drop tablespoonfuls of cream cheese mixture onto pumpkin filling. With knife or small spatula, swirl mixture to give marbled effect.

Bake 50 to 60 minutes or until knife inserted halfway between edge and center comes out clean. Cool completely on wire rack. *Makes 8 servings*

Prep time: 20 minutes
Bake time: 50 minutes, plus cooling

Peanut Butter Crumble Topped Apple Pie

1 cup (8 ounces) dairy sour cream
¾ cup sugar, divided
2 eggs
2 tablespoons plus ¾ cup all-purpose flour, divided
2 teaspoons vanilla extract
¼ teaspoon salt
4 cups peeled, thinly sliced apples (about 5 apples)
1 unbaked 9-inch pie crust
1 cup quick-cooking or regular rolled oats
1 teaspoon ground cinnamon
1 cup REESE'S® Creamy Peanut Butter
1 tablespoon butter or margarine, softened

Heat oven to 350°F. In large bowl, with whisk, blend sour cream, ½ cup sugar, eggs, 2 tablespoons flour, vanilla and salt. Add apples; stir until well coated. Spoon into unbaked crust. Stir together oats, remaining ¾ cup flour, remaining ¼ cup sugar and cinnamon. In small microwave-safe bowl, place peanut butter and butter. Microwave at HIGH (100%) 30 seconds or until butter is melted. Stir mixture until smooth. Add to oat mixture; blend until crumbs are formed. Sprinkle crumb mixture over apples. Bake 55 to 60 minutes or until apples are tender and topping is golden brown. Cool completely on wire rack. Cover; refrigerate leftover pie.
Makes 6 to 8 servings

Pumpkin Cheese-Swirled Pie

Nectarine Pecan Tart

PECAN CRUST

- **1 cup vanilla wafer crumbs**
- **½ cup pecan pieces**
- **2 tablespoons sugar**
- **3 tablespoons unsalted butter, melted**

CREAM CHEESE FILLING

- **1 (8-ounce) package plus 1 (3-ounce) package cream cheese, softened**
- **3 tablespoons sugar**
- **2 tablespoons orange juice**
- **½ teaspoon vanilla**

FRUIT TOPPING

- **2 ripe nectarines**
- **4 tablespoons apricot jelly**

1. For crust, preheat oven to 350°F. Process wafer crumbs, pecans and sugar in food processor until coarse crumbs form. Transfer to small bowl; stir in butter. Pat evenly on bottom and 1 inch up side of 8-inch springform pan. Bake 15 minutes or until lightly browned. Cool completely on wire rack.

2. For filling, beat cream cheese, sugar, juice and vanilla in medium bowl with electric mixer at low speed until blended. Increase speed to high; beat 2 minutes or until fluffy. Pour into crust. Cover; refrigerate 3 hours or until set.

3. For topping, halve and thinly slice nectarines. Arrange over filling.

4. To complete recipe, remove side of pan from tart; place tart on serving platter. Melt jelly in small saucepan, stirring constantly, over low heat. Cool 1 minute. Drizzle jelly over nectarines. Refrigerate, uncovered, until set.

Makes 6 servings

Amaretto Cheesecake Tart

CRUST

- **¾ cup amaretti cookie crumbs**
- **¾ cup zwieback crumbs**
- **1 tablespoon sugar**
- **¼ cup Prune Purée (page 64) or prepared prune butter**

FILLING

- **1 carton (16 ounces) nonfat cottage cheese**
- **4 ounces fat-free cream cheese, softened**
- **2 eggs**
- **2 tablespoons almond-flavored liqueur**

TOPPING & GLAZE

- **2 oranges, peeled and sliced into rounds**
- **1 kiwifruit, peeled and sliced into rounds**
- **2 tablespoons apple jelly, melted**
- **Fresh raspberries, orange peel and mint leaves, for garnish**

Preheat oven to 325°F. To prepare crust, in medium bowl, combine crumbs and sugar. Cut in prune purée with pastry blender until mixture resembles coarse crumbs. Press onto bottom and up side of 9-inch tart pan with removable bottom. To prepare filling, process cottage cheese and cream cheese in food processor 3 to 5 minutes or until smooth. Add eggs and liqueur; process until blended. Pour into prepared crust. Bake in center of oven 30 minutes until filling is set. Cool on wire rack; refrigerate until completely chilled. Arrange fruit on top of filling. Brush fruit with jelly. Garnish with raspberries, orange peel and mint. Cut into wedges.

Makes 10 servings

Favorite recipe from **California Prune Board**

Noreen's Favorite Walnut Pie

- **3 eggs, lightly beaten**
- **1 cup sugar**
- **1 cup dark corn syrup**
- **2 tablespoons all-purpose flour**
- **2 tablespoons butter, melted**
- **1 teaspoon vanilla**
- **1 (9-inch) unbaked pastry pie shell**
- **1½ cups large pieces DIAMOND® Walnuts**

Heat oven to 400°F. Combine eggs, sugar, corn syrup, flour, butter and vanilla; blend well. Pour into unbaked pie shell; arrange walnuts on top. Bake in lower third of oven at 400°F. for 15 minutes. Reduce oven temperature to 350°F.; bake an additional 35 to 45 minutes or until center appears set. Cool completely. *Makes 8 servings*

9-inch Classic Crisco® Double Crust

- **2 cups all-purpose flour**
- **1 teaspoon salt**
- **¾ CRISCO® Stick or ¾ cup CRISCO® all-vegetable shortening**
- **5 tablespoons cold water**

1. Spoon flour into measuring cup and level. Combine flour and salt in medium bowl.

2. Cut in shortening using pastry blender or 2 knives until flour is blended to form pea-size chunks.

3. Sprinkle with water, 1 tablespoon at a time. Toss lightly with fork until dough forms a ball.

4. Divide dough in half. Press half of dough between hands to form a 5- to 6-inch "pancake." Flour rolling surface and rolling pin lightly. Roll dough into circle. Trim circle 1 inch larger than upside-down pie plate. Carefully remove trimmed dough. Set aside to reroll and use for pastry cutout garnish, if desired. Repeat with remaining half of dough.

Makes 2 (9-inch) crusts

Easy-As-Pie Crust

SINGLE PIE CRUST

- **1¼ cups unsifted flour**
- **⅛ teaspoon salt**
- **½ cup MAZOLA® Margarine**
- **2 to 3 tablespoons cold water**

In medium bowl combine flour and salt. With pastry blender or 2 knives, cut in margarine until mixture resembles fine crumbs. Sprinkle water over mixture while tossing to blend well. Press dough firmly into ball. On lightly floured surface, roll into 12-inch circle. Fit loosely into 9-inch pie plate. Trim and flute edge. Fill and bake according to recipe.

Makes one 9-inch crust

BAKING SECRET

To add a shiny golden glaze to the top crust of a fruit pie, brush with milk or an egg wash of 1 beaten egg and 1 tablespoon water just before baking. For a glossier darker color, substitute cream for the milk or an egg yolk for the whole egg. Delay brushing the decorative edge of the pie until the last 15 to 20 minutes of baking to avoid overbrowning.

Early American Pumpkin Pie

1½ cups cooked pumpkin, canned or fresh
1 cup whole or 2% milk
1 cup sugar
2 eggs, beaten
1 tablespoon butter or margarine, melted
½ teaspoon ground cinnamon
¼ teaspoon salt
¼ teaspoon ground ginger
¼ teaspoon ground nutmeg
1 (9-inch) unbaked pie shell
Sweetened whipped cream or whipped topping (optional)
Fresh currants (optional)

Preheat oven to 425°F. Combine pumpkin, milk, sugar, eggs, butter, cinnamon, salt, ginger and nutmeg in large bowl; blend well. Pour into pie shell. Bake 45 to 50 minutes or until knife inserted into filling comes out clean. Cool completely. Serve with whipped cream and garnish with currants, if desired. Refrigerate leftovers.
Makes 6 to 8 servings

Favorite recipe from **Bob Evans Farms®**

Golden Apple Pie with Rum Sauce

Pastry for 2-crust 9-inch pie
6 to 7 Golden Delicious apples
¼ cup firmly packed brown sugar
2 tablespoons all-purpose flour
½ teaspoon ground cinnamon
¼ teaspoon ground nutmeg
¼ teaspoon salt (optional)
¼ cup chopped nuts
Rum Sauce (recipe follows)

Line 9-inch pie plate with half of pastry; reserve remaining pastry. Peel, core and slice apples to equal 7 cups. In large bowl, combine apples, sugar, flour, cinnamon, nutmeg, salt and nuts. Transfer apple mixture to pastry-lined pie plate.

Preheat oven to 425°F. Roll out remaining pastry to 10-inch circle; cut into ¾-inch strips. Arrange strips in lattice pattern on top of apples and trim at edges; pinch edges of crusts together and flute.

Bake 20 minutes. *Reduce oven temperature to 375°F.* Bake 35 to 40 minutes or until apples are tender. If necessary, loosely cover top of pie with foil during baking to prevent overbrowning. Meanwhile, prepare Rum Sauce. To serve, cool pie at least 20 minutes; slice and serve with sauce. *Makes 10 servings*

Rum Sauce: In medium saucepan, combine 1 cup sugar, ¾ cup water and ½ teaspoon ground cinnamon. Bring to a boil over medium-high heat; boil 5 minutes, stirring occasionally. In small bowl, blend 2 tablespoons cornstarch and ¼ cup cold water; gradually stir into hot sugar mixture. Return to heat; cook, stirring constantly, until mixture bubbles and thickens. Remove from heat. Stir in ¼ cup rum. Serve warm.

Favorite recipe from **Washington Apple Commission**

BAKING SECRET

If a pie crust is browning too quickly, cover the edges with strips of foil. An alternative is to cut the bottom out of a foil pie pan and invert it over the pie.

Early American Pumpkin Pie

Country Apple Rhubarb Pie

CRUST

1 (9-inch) Classic CRISCO® Double Crust (page 23)

FILLING

9 cups sliced, peeled Granny Smith apples (about 3 pounds or 6 large apples)
1½ cups chopped (about ½-inch pieces) fresh rhubarb, peeled if tough
¾ cup granulated sugar
½ cup firmly packed light brown sugar
2 tablespoons all-purpose flour
1 tablespoon cornstarch
1 teaspoon ground cinnamon
¼ teaspoon freshly grated nutmeg

GLAZE

1 egg, beaten
1 tablespoon water
1 tablespoon granulated sugar
1 teaspoon ground pecans or walnuts
⅛ teaspoon ground cinnamon

1. For crust, prepare as directed. Roll and press bottom crust into 9- or 9½-inch deep-dish pie plate. *Do not bake.* Heat oven to 425°F.

2. For filling, combine apples and rhubarb in large bowl. Combine ¾ cup granulated sugar, brown sugar, flour, cornstarch, 1 teaspoon cinnamon and nutmeg in medium bowl. Sprinkle over fruit. Toss to coat. Spoon into unbaked pie crust. Moisten pastry edge with water. Cover pie with lattice top, cutting strips 1 inch wide. Flute edge high.

3. For glaze, combine egg and water in small bowl. Brush over crust. Combine remaining glaze ingredients in small bowl. Sprinkle over crust.

4. Bake at 425°F for 20 minutes. *Reduce oven temperature to 350°F.* Bake 30 to 40 minutes or until filling in center is bubbly and crust is golden brown. Place sheet of foil or baking sheet under pie if it starts to bubble over. Cool to room temperature.

Makes 1 (9- or 9½-inch) deep-dish pie

Traditional Cherry Pie

3 cups frozen tart cherries, not thawed
1 cup granulated sugar
2 tablespoons quick-cooking tapioca
½ teaspoon almond extract
Pastry for 2-crust (double) 9-inch pie
2 tablespoons butter or margarine

Preheat oven to 400°F. In medium bowl, combine cherries, sugar, tapioca and almond extract; mix well. Let cherry mixture stand 15 minutes.

Line 9-inch pie plate with 1 pastry crust; fill with cherry mixture. Dot with butter. Cover with top crust. Cut slits for steam to escape. Seal edges and flute.

Bake 50 to 55 minutes or until crust is golden brown and filling is bubbly.

Makes 6 to 8 servings

Favorite recipe from **Cherry Marketing Institute, Inc.**

Country Apple Rhubarb Pie

Heavenly Brownies & Bars

Rich chocolaty brownies and sensational bar cookies have always been a special part of picnics and parties. With this collection of wonderful recipes, discover just how easy it is to serve those treats to your family.

Moist and Minty Brownies

1¼ cups all-purpose flour
½ teaspoon baking soda
¼ teaspoon salt
¾ cup granulated sugar
½ cup (1 stick) butter or margarine
2 tablespoons water
1½ cups (10-ounce package) NESTLÉ® TOLL HOUSE® Mint-Chocolate Morsels, *divided*
1 teaspoon vanilla extract
2 eggs

COMBINE flour, baking soda and salt in small bowl. Combine sugar, butter and water in medium microwave-safe bowl. Microwave on HIGH (100%) power for 3 minutes, stirring halfway through cooking time. Stir until smooth. Add *1 cup* morsels and vanilla; stir until smooth. Add eggs, one at a time, stirring well after each addition. Stir in flour mixture and *remaining* morsels. Spread into greased 9-inch square baking pan.

BAKE in preheated 350°F. oven for 20 to 30 minutes or until center is set. Cool in pan on wire rack (center will sink).

Makes about 16 brownies

Saucepan method: COMBINE sugar, butter and water in medium saucepan. Bring *just to a boil* over medium heat, stirring constantly; remove from heat. Add *1 cup* morsels and vanilla; stir until smooth. Add eggs one at a time, stirring well after each addition. Stir in flour mixture and *remaining* morsels. Spread in pan; bake as directed above.

Moist and Minty Brownies

BAKING SECRET

For an easy glaze for bar cookies, sprinkle them with chocolate chips immediately after baking, then cover with foil. After 3 or 4 minutes, remove the foil and spread the melted chips over the bars.

Cherry Cheesecake Squares

- **2 cups graham cracker crumbs**
- **1 cup sugar, divided**
- **¼ cup (½ stick) butter or margarine, melted**
- **3 packages (8 ounces each) PHILADELPHIA BRAND® Cream Cheese, softened**
- **1 teaspoon vanilla**
- **2 eggs**
- **1 can (20 ounces) cherry pie filling**

MIX crumbs, ¼ cup sugar and butter. Press into 13×9-inch baking pan. Bake at 325°F for 10 minutes.

MIX cream cheese, remaining ¾ cup sugar and vanilla with electric mixer on medium speed until well blended. Add eggs; mix just until blended. Pour over crust.

BAKE at 325°F for 35 minutes or until center is almost set. Cool. Refrigerate 3 hours or overnight. Top with pie filling. Cut into squares. Garnish, if desired.

Makes 18 squares

Prep time: 20 minutes plus refrigerating
Bake time: 35 minutes

Old-Fashioned Brownies

- **3 ounces (3 squares) unsweetened chocolate**
- **½ cup shortening**
- **1½ cups sugar**
- **3 eggs**
- **1½ teaspoons vanilla**
- **¼ teaspoon salt**
- **1 cup all-purpose flour**
- **1½ cups chopped DIAMOND® Walnuts**

VELVET CHOCOLATE ICING (OPTIONAL)

- **1 ounce (1 square) unsweetened chocolate, melted**
- **2 tablespoons butter**
- **2 tablespoons light corn syrup**
- **1 cup powdered sugar**
- **1 tablespoon milk**
- **1 teaspoon vanilla**

Heat oven to 325°F. Grease an 8-inch square baking pan. In top of double boiler over hot, not boiling, water, melt chocolate and shortening. Cool slightly. Combine sugar, eggs, vanilla and salt in large bowl; blend in chocolate mixture. Stir in flour; fold in walnuts. Spread in greased pan. Bake at 325°F. for about 40 minutes (brownies should still be soft). Cool completely in pan. If desired, prepare Velvet Chocolate Icing. Combine chocolate, butter and corn syrup; blend well. Add powdered sugar, milk and vanilla; blend well. Spread over brownies; cut into bars. *Makes 20 brownies*

Variation: Spread a thin layer of raspberry jam over top of hot brownies. Cool before spreading with icing.

Cherry Cheesecake Squares

Toffee Bars

1 cup butter or margarine, softened
1 cup firmly packed brown sugar
1 egg yolk
1 teaspoon vanilla
2 cups all-purpose flour
1 cup chopped DIAMOND® Walnuts, divided
½ cup semi-sweet chocolate pieces

Heat oven to 350°F. Grease 13×9-inch pan. Combine butter, brown sugar, egg yolk and vanilla; beat until light and fluffy. Stir in flour and ***½ cup*** walnuts; spread in prepared pan. Bake at 350°F. for 25 minutes or until lightly browned. Immediately sprinkle with chocolate; spread over base when melted. Sprinkle chocolate with remaining ½ cup walnuts. Cool completely; cut into bars.

Makes 24 bars

P.B. Chips Brownie Cups

1 cup (2 sticks) butter or margarine
2 cups sugar
2 teaspoons vanilla extract
4 eggs
¾ cup HERSHEY'S® Cocoa or HERSHEY'S® European Style Cocoa
1¾ cups all-purpose flour
½ teaspoon baking powder
½ teaspoon salt
1⅔ cups (10-ounce package) REESE'S® Peanut Butter Chips, divided

1. Heat oven to 350°F. Line 18 muffin cups (2½ inches in diameter) with paper or foil bake cups.

2. In large microwave-safe bowl, place butter. Microwave at HIGH (100%) 1 to 1½ minutes or until melted. Stir in sugar and vanilla. Add eggs; beat well. Add cocoa; beat until well blended. Add flour, baking powder and salt; beat well. Stir in 1⅓ cups peanut butter chips. Divide batter evenly into muffin cups; sprinkle with remaining ⅓ cup peanut butter chips.

3. Bake 25 to 30 minutes or until surface is firm; cool completely in pan on wire rack.

Makes about 18 brownie cups

Bittersweet Brownies

MAZOLA® No Stick Cooking Spray
4 squares (1 ounce each) unsweetened chocolate, melted
1 cup sugar
½ cup HELLMANN'S® or BEST FOODS® Real or Light Mayonnaise or Low Fat Mayonnaise Dressing
2 eggs
1 teaspoon vanilla
¾ cup flour
½ teaspoon baking powder
¼ teaspoon salt
½ cup chopped walnuts

Preheat oven to 350°F. Spray 8×8×2-inch baking pan with cooking spray. In large bowl, stir chocolate, sugar, mayonnaise, eggs and vanilla until smooth. Stir in flour, baking powder and salt until well blended. Stir in walnuts. Spread in prepared pan.

Bake 25 to 30 minutes or until wooden pick inserted into center comes out clean. Cool in pan on wire rack. Cut into 2-inch squares.

Makes 16 brownies

Brownie Kiss Cups

Brownie Kiss Cups

- 1 package (19.8 ounces) DUNCAN HINES® Chewy Fudge Brownie Mix
- 1 egg
- ⅓ cup water
- ⅓ cup CRISCO® Oil or CRISCO® PURITAN® Canola Oil
- 25 milk chocolate candy kisses, unwrapped

1. Preheat oven to 350°F. Place 25 (2-inch) foil liners in muffin pans or on cookie sheets.

2. Combine brownie mix, egg, water and oil in large bowl. Stir with spoon until well blended, about 50 strokes. Fill each liner with 2 measuring tablespoonfuls batter. Bake at 350°F for 17 to 20 minutes. Remove from oven. Place 1 milk chocolate candy kiss on each cupcake. Bake 1 minute longer. Cool 5 to 10 minutes in pans. Remove to cooling racks. Cool completely. *Makes 25 brownie cups*

BAKING SECRET

For easy removal of brownies and bar cookies (and no cleanup!), line the baking pan with foil and leave at least 3 inches hanging over on each end. Place the brownies or bars on a cutting board, remove the foil and cut the treats into pieces.

Nutty Chocolate Caramel Bars

2⅓ cups all-purpose flour, divided
2 cups rolled oats
1 cup firmly packed brown sugar
1 teaspoon baking soda
¼ teaspoon salt
1 cup butter or margarine, melted
2 cups (12-ounce package) semi-sweet chocolate pieces
1½ cups chopped DIAMOND® Walnuts
1 (12.25-ounce jar) caramel ice cream topping

Heat oven to 350°F. Combine ***2 cups*** flour, oats, brown sugar, baking soda and salt. Stir in butter; mix well. Reserve ***1 cup*** crumb mixture; press remainder into ungreased 13×9-inch pan. Bake at 350°F. for 15 minutes or until lightly browned. Remove from oven; sprinkle with chocolate and walnuts. Combine caramel topping and remaining ⅓ cup flour; drizzle over chocolate and walnuts. Sprinkle with reserved crumb mixture. Return to oven; bake additional 20 minutes or until lightly browned. Cool completely; cut into bars.

Makes 32 bars

One Bowl™ Brownies

4 squares BAKER'S® Unsweetened Chocolate
¾ cup (1½ sticks) margarine or butter
2 cups sugar
3 eggs
1 teaspoon vanilla
1 cup all-purpose flour
1 cup chopped nuts (optional)

PREHEAT oven to 350°F.

MICROWAVE chocolate and margarine in large microwavable bowl on HIGH 2 minutes or until margarine is melted. **Stir until chocolate is completely melted.**

STIR sugar into melted chocolate mixture. Mix in eggs and vanilla until well blended. Stir in flour and nuts. Spread in greased foil-lined 13×9-inch pan.

BAKE for 30 to 35 minutes or until toothpick inserted into center comes out with fudgy crumbs. **Do not overbake.** Cool in pan; cut into squares.

Makes 24 brownies

Prep time: 10 minutes
Bake time: 30 to 35 minutes

Peanut Butter Swirl Brownies: Prepare One Bowl™ Brownie batter as directed, reserving 1 tablespoon of the margarine and 2 tablespoons of the sugar. Add reserved ingredients to ⅔ cup peanut butter; mix well.

Place spoonfuls of peanut butter mixture over brownie batter. Swirl with knife to marbleize. Bake for 30 to 35 minutes or until toothpick inserted into center comes out with fudgy crumbs. Cool in pan; cut into squares. Makes about 24 brownies.

Prep time: 15 minutes
Bake time: 30 to 35 minutes

Rocky Road Brownies: Prepare One Bowl™ Brownies as directed. Bake for 30 minutes. Immediately sprinkle 2 cups miniature marshmallows, 1 cup BAKER'S® Semi-Sweet Real Chocolate Chips and 1 cup chopped nuts over brownies immediately. Continue baking 3 to 5 minutes or until topping begins to melt together. Cool in pan; cut into squares. Makes about 24 brownies.

Prep time: 15 minutes
Bake time: 35 minutes

Chocolate Raspberry Streusel Squares

1½ cups all-purpose flour
1½ cups QUAKER® Oats (quick or old fashioned, uncooked)
½ cup granulated sugar
½ cup firmly packed brown sugar
1 teaspoon baking powder
¼ teaspoon salt (optional)
1 cup (2 sticks) margarine or butter, chilled and cut into pieces
1 cup raspberry preserves or jam (about 10 ounces)
1 cup (6 ounces) semisweet chocolate pieces
¼ cup chopped almonds
½ cup (3 ounces) semisweet chocolate pieces *or* 1 bar (4 ounces) white chocolate, chopped and melted* (optional)

*To melt chocolate: Place in dry glass measuring cup or microwaveable bowl. Microwave at HIGH 1 to 2 minutes, stirring every 30 seconds until smooth. Or, place in top part of dry double boiler over hot, not boiling, water; stir occasionally until smooth.

Heat oven to 375°F. In large bowl, combine flour, oats, sugars, baking powder and salt. Cut in margarine with pastry blender or two knives until mixture is crumbly. Reserve 1 cup oat mixture for streusel; set aside. Press remaining oat mixture onto bottom of ungreased 9-inch square baking pan. Bake 10 minutes. Spread preserves over crust; sprinkle evenly with chocolate pieces. Combine reserved oat mixture and almonds; sprinkle over chocolate pieces, patting gently. Bake 30 to 35 minutes or until golden brown. Cool completely. Drizzle with melted chocolate, if desired. Let chocolate set before cutting into bars. Store tightly covered. *Makes 36 bars*

Peanut Butter Marbled Brownies

4 ounces cream cheese, softened
½ cup peanut butter
2 tablespoons sugar
1 egg
1 package (20 to 22 ounces) brownie mix plus ingredients to prepare mix
¾ cup lightly salted cocktail peanuts

1. Preheat oven to 350°F. Lightly grease 13×9-inch baking pan; set aside.

2. Beat cream cheese, peanut butter, sugar and egg in medium bowl with electric mixer at medium speed until blended; set aside.

3. Prepare brownie mix according to package directions. Spread evenly in prepared pan. Spoon peanut butter mixture in dollops over brownie mixture. Swirl peanut butter mixture into brownie mixture with tip of knife. Sprinkle peanuts on top; lightly press peanuts down.

4. Bake 30 to 35 minutes or until wooden pick inserted into center comes out almost clean. *Do not overbake.* Cool brownies completely in pan on wire rack. Cut into 2-inch squares. *Makes 24 brownies*

BAKING SECRET

Replacing the margarine or butter in a recipe with a spread, diet margarine, whipped margarine or whipped butter may result in an inferior baked product. For best results, use the product called for in the recipe.

Orange Coconut Cream Bars

1 18¼-ounce package yellow cake mix
1 cup quick-cooking or old-fashioned oats, uncooked
¾ cup chopped nuts
½ cup butter or margarine, melted
1 large egg
1 14-ounce can sweetened condensed milk
2 teaspoons grated orange zest
1 cup shredded coconut
1 cup "M & M's"® Semi-Sweet Chocolate Mini Baking Bits

Preheat oven to 375°F. Lightly grease 13×9×2-inch baking pan; set aside. In large bowl combine cake mix, oats, nuts, butter and egg until ingredients are thoroughly moistened and mixture resembles coarse crumbs. Reserve 1 cup mixture. Firmly press remaining mixture onto bottom of prepared pan; bake 10 minutes. In separate bowl combine condensed milk and orange zest; spread over baked base. Combine reserved crumb mixture, coconut and "M & M's"® Semi-Sweet Chocolate Mini Baking Bits; sprinkle evenly over condensed milk mixture and press in lightly. Continue baking 20 to 25 minutes or until golden brown. Cool completely. Cut into bars. Store in tightly covered container.

Makes 26 bars

Praline Bars

¾ cup (1½ sticks) butter or margarine, softened
1 cup sugar, divided
1 teaspoon vanilla, divided
1½ cups flour
2 packages (8 ounces each) PHILADELPHIA BRAND® Cream Cheese, softened
2 eggs
½ cup almond brickle chips
3 tablespoons caramel ice cream topping

MIX butter, ½ cup of the sugar and ½ teaspoon of the vanilla with electric mixer on medium speed until light and fluffy. Gradually add flour, mixing on low speed until blended. Press onto bottom of 13×9-inch baking pan. Bake at 350°F for 20 to 23 minutes or until lightly browned.

MIX cream cheese, remaining ½ cup sugar and ½ teaspoon vanilla with electric mixer on medium speed until well blended. Add eggs; mix well. Blend in chips. Pour over crust. Dot top of cream cheese mixture with topping. Cut through batter with knife several times for marble effect.

BAKE at 350°F for 30 minutes. Cool in pan on wire rack. Refrigerate. Cut into bars.

Makes 24 bars

Prep time: 30 minutes
Bake time: 30 minutes

Orange Coconut Cream Bars

Brownie Caramel Pecan Bars

- ½ cup sugar
- 2 tablespoons butter or margarine
- 2 tablespoons water
- 2 cups (12-ounce package) HERSHEY'S® Semi-Sweet Chocolate Chips, divided
- 2 eggs
- 1 teaspoon vanilla extract
- ⅔ cup all-purpose flour
- ¼ teaspoon baking soda
- ¼ teaspoon salt
- Caramel Topping (recipe follows)
- 1 cup pecan pieces

1. Heat oven to 350°F. Line 9-inch square baking pan with foil, extending foil over edges of pan. Grease and flour foil.

2. In medium saucepan, combine sugar, butter and water; cook over low heat, stirring constantly, until mixture boils. Remove from heat. Immediately add 1 cup chocolate chips; stir until melted. Beat in eggs and vanilla until well blended. Stir together flour, baking soda and salt; stir into chocolate mixture. Spread batter into prepared pan.

3. Bake 15 to 20 minutes or until brownies begin to pull away from sides of pan. Meanwhile, prepare Caramel Topping. Remove brownies from oven; immediately and carefully spread with prepared topping. Sprinkle remaining 1 cup chips and pecans over topping. Cool completely in pan on wire rack, being careful not to disturb chips while soft. Lift out of pan. Cut into bars. *Makes about 16 bars*

Caramel Topping: Remove wrappers from 25 caramels. In medium microwave-safe bowl, place ¼ cup (½ stick) butter or margarine, caramels and 2 tablespoons milk. Microwave at HIGH (100%) 1 minute; stir. Microwave an additional 1 to 2 minutes, stirring every 30 seconds, or until caramels are melted and mixture is smooth when stirred. Use immediately.

Double Decadence Chocolate Chip Brownies

- 1 cup granulated sugar
- ⅔ cup (1 stick and 3 tablespoons) margarine or butter, softened
- 2 eggs
- 1 teaspoon vanilla
- 2 cups (12-ounce package) semi-sweet chocolate pieces, divided
- 1¼ cups all-purpose flour
- 1 cup QUAKER® Oats (quick or old fashioned, uncooked)
- 1 teaspoon baking powder
- ½ cup chopped nuts (optional)
- Powdered sugar

HEAT oven to 350°F. **LIGHTLY** grease 13×9-inch baking pan. **BEAT** sugar, margarine, eggs and vanilla until smooth. **ADD** 1 cup chocolate, melted;* mix well. **ADD** flour, oats, baking powder, remaining 1 cup chocolate pieces and nuts, mixing well. **SPREAD** into prepared pan. **BAKE** 25 to 30 minutes or until brownies pull away from sides of pan. **COOL** completely. Sprinkle with powdered sugar, if desired. Cut into bars. *Makes 24 brownies*

*To melt 1 cup chocolate pieces: Microwave at HIGH 1 to 2 minutes, stirring every 30 seconds until smooth. Or, heat in heavy saucepan over low heat, stirring until smooth.

Brownie Caramel Pecan Bars

Mini Kisses® Praline Bars

2 cups all-purpose flour
1⅓ cups packed light brown sugar, divided
½ cup (1 stick) plus ⅔ cup butter, divided
1 cup coarsely chopped pecans
1¾ cups (10-ounce package) HERSHEY'S® MINI KISSES® Chocolate

1. Heat oven to 350°F.

2. In large bowl, stir together flour and 1 cup brown sugar; cut in ½ cup butter with pastry blender until fine crumbs form. Press mixture into 13×9×2-inch baking pan; sprinkle with pecans.

3. In small saucepan, place remaining ⅔ cup butter and remaining ⅓ cup brown sugar; cook over medium heat, stirring constantly, until mixture boils. Continue boiling, stirring constantly, 30 seconds, until sugar dissolves; drizzle evenly over pecans and crust.

4. Bake 18 to 22 minutes until topping is bubbly and golden; remove from oven. Immediately sprinkle Mini Kisses Chocolate over top. Cool completely in pan on wire rack. Cut into bars.

Makes about 36 bars

Mini Kisses® Praline Bars

BAKING SECRET

Toasting nuts enhances their flavor. Simply spread nuts in a single layer on a jelly-roll pan and bake in a preheated 325°F oven for 8 to 10 minutes or until lightly toasted, stirring several times. Cool the nuts before using them.

Almond Toffee Bars

- **¾ cup plus 1 tablespoon butter, softened and divided**
- **¾ cup firmly packed brown sugar**
- **1 egg yolk**
- **½ teaspoon almond extract**
- **½ teaspoon vanilla extract**
- **1½ cups all-purpose flour**
- **¼ teaspoon salt**
- **1 package (12 ounces) semi-sweet chocolate chips**
- **¾ cup BLUE DIAMOND® Chopped Natural Almonds, toasted**

Cream ¾ cup butter and sugar; beat in egg yolk and extracts, mixing well. Blend in flour and salt. Spread dough evenly onto bottom of ungreased 13×9×2-inch baking pan. Bake at 350°F. for 25 minutes or until golden brown. Melt chocolate in double boiler over simmering water. Remove from heat and add remaining 1 tablespoon butter. Beat until chocolate is glossy. Spread over baked crust and sprinkle with almonds. Cool to allow chocolate to set. Cut into bars. *Makes about 35 bars*

Pecan Pie Bars

- **¾ cup butter or margarine**
- **½ cup powdered sugar**
- **1½ cups all-purpose flour**
- **3 eggs**
- **2 cups coarsely chopped pecans**
- **1 cup granulated sugar**
- **1 cup light corn syrup**
- **2 tablespoons butter or margarine, melted**
- **1 teaspoon vanilla**

1. Preheat oven to 350°F.

2. For crust, beat ¾ cup butter in large bowl with electric mixer at medium speed until smooth. Add powdered sugar; beat until well blended. Add flour gradually, beating at low speed after each addition. (Mixture will be crumbly but will press together easily.)

3. Press dough evenly into *ungreased* 13×9-inch baking pan. Press mixture slightly up sides of pan (less than ¼ inch) to form lip to hold filling. Bake 20 to 25 minutes or until golden brown.

4. Meanwhile, for filling, beat eggs lightly in medium bowl with fork. Add pecans, granulated sugar, corn syrup, melted butter and vanilla; mix well. Pour filling over partially baked crust.

5. Return to oven; bake 35 to 40 minutes or until filling is set. Loosen edges with knife. Cool completely on wire rack before cutting into squares. Cover and refrigerate until 10 to 15 minutes before serving time. *Do not freeze.* *Makes about 48 bars*

Currant Cheesecake Bars

- **½ cup butter or margarine, softened**
- **1 cup all-purpose flour**
- **½ cup packed light brown sugar**
- **½ cup finely chopped pecans**
- **1 package (8 ounces) cream cheese, softened**
- **¼ cup granulated sugar**
- **1 egg**
- **1 tablespoon milk**
- **2 teaspoons grated lemon peel**
- **⅓ cup currant jelly or seedless raspberry jam**

1. Preheat oven to 350°F. Grease 9-inch square baking pan. Beat butter in medium bowl with electric mixer at medium speed until smooth. Add flour, brown sugar and pecans; beat at low speed until well blended. Press mixture into bottom and partially up sides of prepared pan.

2. Bake about 15 minutes or until light brown. If sides of crust have shrunk down, press back up and reshape with spoon. Cool 5 minutes on wire rack.

3. Meanwhile, beat cream cheese in large bowl with electric mixer at medium speed until smooth. Add granulated sugar, egg, milk and lemon peel; beat until well blended.

4. Heat jelly in small saucepan over low heat 2 to 3 minutes or until smooth, stirring occasionally.

5. Pour cream cheese mixture over crust. Drizzle jelly in 7 to 8 strips across filling with spoon. Swirl jelly through filling with knife to create marbled effect.

6. Return pan to oven; bake 20 to 25 minutes or until filling is set. Cool completely on wire rack before cutting into bars. Store in airtight container in refrigerator up to 1 week.

Makes about 32 bars

BAKING SECRET

When melting chocolate, avoid high heat because chocolate scorches easily.

Fudgy Chocolate Mint Oatmeal Squares

- **1¼ cups all-purpose flour**
- **½ teaspoon baking soda**
- **1 cup packed brown sugar**
- **½ cup (1 stick) butter or margarine, softened**
- **1 egg**
- **1½ cups quick or old-fashioned oats**
- **1 cup chopped nuts**
- **1½ cups (10-ounce package) NESTLÉ® TOLL HOUSE® Mint-Chocolate Morsels**
- **1¼ cups (14-ounce can) CARNATION® Sweetened Condensed Milk**
- **2 tablespoons butter or margarine**

COMBINE flour and baking soda in small bowl. Beat sugar and *½ cup* butter in large mixer bowl until creamy. Beat in egg. Gradually beat in flour mixture. Stir in oats and nuts. Press *2 cups* oat mixture onto bottom of greased 13×9-inch baking pan.

MELT morsels, sweetened condensed milk and *2 tablespoons* butter in heavy saucepan over low heat, stirring constantly until smooth; pour over crust. Crumble *remaining* oat mixture over filling.

BAKE in preheated 350°F. oven for 25 to 30 minutes or until filling is set and topping begins to brown. Cool in pan on wire rack.

Makes about 30 squares

Currant Cheesecake Bars

Kid-Pleasing Cookies

Remember Mom's cookie jar? Always nestled in its own spot in the kitchen, the cookie jar overflowed with your favorite treats. Continue that never-forgotten tradition for your children and their friends with this selection of kid-pleasing cookies.

Original Nestlé® Toll House® Chocolate Chip Cookies

2¼ cups all-purpose flour
1 teaspoon baking soda
1 teaspoon salt
1 cup (2 sticks) butter, softened
¾ cup granulated sugar
¾ cup packed brown sugar
1 teaspoon vanilla extract
2 eggs
2 cups (12-ounce package) NESTLÉ® TOLL HOUSE® Semi-Sweet Chocolate Morsels
1 cup chopped nuts

COMBINE flour, baking soda and salt in small bowl; set aside.

BEAT butter, granulated sugar, brown sugar and vanilla extract in large bowl until creamy. Beat in eggs. Gradually beat in flour mixture. Stir in morsels and nuts.

Drop by rounded measuring tablespoonfuls onto ungreased cookie sheets.

BAKE in preheated 375°F. oven 9 to 11 minutes or until edges are golden brown. Cool on cookie sheets for 2 minutes. Remove from cookie sheets; cool completely on wire racks.

Makes about 5 dozen cookies

Pan Cookies: PREPARE dough as directed above. Spread dough in greased 15½×10½×1-inch jelly-roll pan. Bake in preheated 375°F. oven for 20 to 25 minutes. Cool completely in pan on wire rack. Cut into 2-inch squares. Makes about 35 squares.

Original Nestlé® Toll House® Chocolate Chip Cookies

Black and White Cut-Outs

- **1 cup butter or margarine, softened**
- **¾ cup granulated sugar**
- **¾ cup packed light brown sugar**
- **2 eggs**
- **1 teaspoon vanilla**
- **2¾ cups plus 2 tablespoons all-purpose flour, divided**
- **1 teaspoon baking soda**
- **¾ teaspoon salt**
- **¼ cup unsweetened cocoa powder**
- **1 white baking bar (4 ounces), broken into ½-inch pieces**
- **4 ounces semisweet chocolate chips**
- **Assorted decorative candies (optional)**

Beat butter, granulated sugar and brown sugar in large bowl until light and fluffy. Beat in eggs, 1 at a time. Beat in vanilla. Combine 2¾ cups flour, baking soda and salt in medium bowl; add to butter mixture. Beat until well blended. Remove half of dough from bowl; reserve. To make chocolate dough, beat cocoa into remaining dough with spoon until well blended. To make butter cookie dough, beat remaining 2 tablespoons flour into reserved dough. Flatten each half of dough into a disc; wrap in plastic wrap and refrigerate about 1½ hours or until firm.

Preheat oven to 375°F. Working with one dough at a time, place on lightly floured surface. Roll out dough to ¼-inch thickness. Cut into desired shapes with cookie cutters. Place cookies 1 inch apart on ungreased cookie sheets. Bake 9 to 11 minutes or until set. Let cookies stand on cookie sheets 2 minutes. Remove cookies to wire racks; cool completely.

For white chocolate drizzle, place baking bar pieces in small heavy resealable plastic bag; seal bag. Microwave at MEDIUM (50% power) 2 minutes. Turn bag over; heat at MEDIUM 2 to 3 minutes or until melted. Knead bag until white chocolate is smooth. Cut small corner from bag; pipe or drizzle melted chocolate onto chocolate cookies. Decorate as desired with assorted candies. Let stand until white chocolate is set, about 30 minutes.

For chocolate drizzle, place chocolate chips in small heavy resealable plastic bag; seal bag. Microwave at HIGH 1 minute. Turn bag over; heat at HIGH 1 to 2 minutes or until chocolate is melted. Knead bag until chocolate is smooth. Cut small corner from bag; pipe or drizzle chocolate onto butter cookies. Decorate as desired with assorted candies. Let stand until chocolate is set, about 40 minutes.

Makes 3 to 4 dozen cookies

Black and White Sandwiches: Cut cookies out with cookie cutter. Bake according to above directions. Spread thin layer of prepared frosting on bottom side of chocolate cookie. Place bottom side of butter cookie over frosting. Drizzle either side of cookie with melted chocolate or white chocolate.

BAKING SECRET

For easy cleanup when rolling cookie dough, roll out the dough on a sheet of waxed paper that has been placed right on the countertop. To prevent the waxed paper from sliding, lightly spray the countertop under it with water.

Maple Walnut Cookies

Maple Walnut Cookies

1¼ cups firmly packed light brown sugar
¾ Butter Flavor CRISCO® Stick or ¾ cup Butter Flavor CRISCO® all-vegetable shortening
2 tablespoons maple syrup
1 teaspoon vanilla
1 teaspoon maple extract
1 egg
1¾ cups all-purpose flour
1 teaspoon salt
¾ teaspoon baking soda
½ teaspoon cinnamon
1½ cups chopped walnuts
30 to 40 walnut halves

1. Heat oven to 375°F. Place sheets of foil on countertop for cooling cookies.

2. Place brown sugar, shortening, maple syrup, vanilla and maple extract in large bowl. Beat at medium speed of electric mixer until well blended. Add egg; beat well.

3. Combine flour, salt, baking soda and cinnamon. Add to shortening mixture; beat at low speed just until blended. Stir in chopped walnuts.

4. Drop dough by rounded measuring tablespoonfuls 3 inches apart onto ungreased cookie sheets. Press walnut half into center of each cookie.

5. Bake one cookie sheet at a time at 375°F for 8 to 10 minutes for chewy cookies, or 11 to 13 minutes for crisp cookies. *Do not overbake.* Cool 2 minutes on baking sheet. Remove cookies to foil to cool completely.

Makes about 3 dozen cookies

Moravian Spice Crisps

- **⅓ cup shortening**
- **⅓ cup packed brown sugar**
- **¼ cup unsulfured molasses**
- **¼ cup dark corn syrup**
- **1¾ to 2 cups all-purpose flour, divided**
- **2 teaspoons ground ginger**
- **1¼ teaspoons baking soda**
- **1 teaspoon ground cinnamon**
- **½ teaspoon ground cloves**
- **Powdered sugar**

1. Melt shortening in small saucepan over low heat. Remove from heat; stir in brown sugar, molasses and corn syrup. Cool.

2. Combine 1½ cups flour, ginger, baking soda, cinnamon and cloves in large bowl. Beat in shortening mixture with electric mixer at medium speed. Beat in additional flour until stiff dough forms.

3. Knead dough on lightly floured surface, adding more flour if too sticky. Form dough into 2 discs; wrap in plastic wrap and refrigerate 30 minutes or until firm.

4. Preheat oven to 350°F. Grease cookie sheets; set aside. Working with 1 disc at a time, unwrap dough and place on lightly floured surface. Roll out dough with lightly floured rolling pin to 1⁄16-inch thickness.

5. Cut dough with floured 2⅜-inch scalloped cookie cutter. (If dough becomes too soft, refrigerate several minutes before continuing.) Gently press dough trimmings together; reroll and cut out more cookies. Place cookies ½ inch apart on prepared cookie sheets.

6. Bake 8 minutes or until firm. Remove cookies to wire racks; cool completely.

7. Place small strips of cardboard or parchment paper over cookies; dust with sifted powdered sugar. Carefully remove cardboard.

Makes about 6 dozen cookies

BAKING SECRET

Never store two kinds of cookies in the same container, because their flavors and textures can change.

Soft Spicy Molasses Cookies

- **2 cups all-purpose flour**
- **1 cup sugar**
- **¾ cup margarine or butter, softened**
- **⅓ cup light molasses**
- **3 tablespoons milk**
- **1 egg**
- **½ teaspoon baking soda**
- **½ teaspoon ground ginger**
- **½ teaspoon ground cinnamon**
- **½ teaspoon ground cloves**
- **⅛ teaspoon salt**
- **Sugar for rolling**

Combine flour, 1 cup sugar, margarine, molasses, milk, egg, baking soda, ginger, cinnamon, cloves and salt in large bowl. Beat at low speed of electric mixer, 2 to 3 minutes. Cover; refrigerate until firm enough to handle, at least 4 hours or overnight.

Preheat oven to 350°F. Shape dough into 1-inch balls; roll in sugar. Place 2 inches apart on ungreased cookie sheets. Bake 9 to 12 minutes or until just firm to the touch. Remove immediately to wire racks to cool. *Makes about 4 dozen cookies*

Moravian Spice Crisps

Peanut Butter Thumbprints

- 1¼ cups firmly packed light brown sugar
- ¾ cup creamy peanut butter
- ½ CRISCO® Stick or ½ cup CRISCO® all-vegetable shortening
- 3 tablespoons milk
- 1 tablespoon vanilla
- 1 egg
- 1¾ cups all-purpose flour
- ¾ teaspoon baking soda
- ¾ teaspoon salt
- Granulated sugar
- ¼ cup strawberry jam,* stirred

*Substitute your favorite jam or jelly for strawberry jam.

1. Heat oven to 375°F. Place sheets of foil on countertop for cooling cookies.

2. Place brown sugar, peanut butter, shortening, milk and vanilla in large bowl. Beat at medium speed of electric mixer until well blended. Add egg; beat just until blended.

3. Combine flour, baking soda and salt. Add to shortening mixture; beat at low speed just until blended.

4. Shape dough into 1-inch balls. Roll in granulated sugar. Place 2 inches apart on ungreased cookie sheets.

5. Bake one cookie sheet at a time at 375°F for 6 minutes. Press centers of cookies immediately with back of measuring teaspoon. Bake 3 minutes longer or until cookies are set and just beginning to brown. *Do not overbake.* Cool 2 minutes on baking sheet. Spoon jam into center of each cookie. Remove cookies to foil to cool completely.

Makes about 4 dozen cookies

Crispy Oat Drops

- 1 cup (2 sticks) butter or margarine, softened
- ½ cup granulated sugar
- ½ cup firmly packed light brown sugar
- 1 large egg
- 2 cups all-purpose flour
- ½ cup quick-cooking or old-fashioned oats, uncooked
- 1 teaspoon cream of tartar
- ½ teaspoon baking soda
- ¼ teaspoon salt
- 1¾ cups "M & M's"® Semi-Sweet Chocolate Mini Baking Bits
- 1 cup toasted rice cereal
- ½ cup shredded coconut
- ½ cup coarsely chopped pecans

Preheat oven to 350°F. In large bowl cream butter and sugars until light and fluffy; beat in egg. In medium bowl combine flour, oats, cream of tartar, baking soda and salt; blend flour mixture into creamed mixture. Stir in "M & M's"® Semi-Sweet Chocolate Mini Baking Bits, cereal, coconut and pecans. Drop by heaping tablespoonfuls about 2 inches apart onto ungreased cookie sheets. Bake 10 to 13 minutes or until lightly browned. Cool completely on wire racks. Store in tightly covered container.

Makes about 4 dozen cookies

BAKING SECRET

For more uniformly shaped drop cookies, scoop dough using a small ice cream scoop with a release bar. The handiest sizes are 40, 50 and 80.

Molded Scotch Shortbread

1½ cups all-purpose flour
¼ teaspoon salt
¾ cup butter, softened
⅓ cup sugar
1 large egg
10-inch diameter ceramic shortbread mold

1. Preheat oven to temperature recommended by shortbread mold manufacturer. Place flour and salt in medium bowl; stir to combine.

2. Beat butter and sugar in large bowl with electric mixer at medium speed until light and fluffy. Beat in egg. Gradually add flour mixture. Beat at low speed until well blended.

3. Spray shortbread mold with nonstick cooking spray. Press dough firmly into mold. Bake, cool and remove from mold according to manufacturer's directions.

4. If mold is not available, preheat oven to 350°F. Roll tablespoonfuls of dough into 1-inch balls. Place balls 2 inches apart on *ungreased* cookie sheet; press with fork to flatten.

5. Bake 18 to 20 minutes or until edges are lightly browned. Let cookies stand on cookie sheet 2 minutes. Remove cookies with spatula to wire rack; cool completely.

6. Store cookies tightly covered at room temperature or freeze up to 3 months.

Makes 1 shortbread mold or 2 dozen cookies

BAKING SECRET

When reusing cookie sheets for several batches of cookies, cool the sheets completely before placing dough on them. The dough will soften and begin to spread on a hot baking sheet.

Fudgy Peanut Butter Jiffy Cookies

2 cups granulated sugar
½ cup evaporated milk
½ cup (1 stick) margarine or butter
¼ cup unsweetened cocoa powder
2½ cups QUAKER® Oats (quick or old fashioned, uncooked)
½ cup peanut butter
½ cup raisins or chopped dates
2 teaspoons vanilla

In large saucepan, combine sugar, milk, margarine and cocoa. Bring to a boil over medium heat, stirring frequently. Continue boiling 3 minutes. Remove from heat. Stir in oats, peanut butter, raisins and vanilla; mix well. Quickly drop by tablespoonfuls onto waxed paper or greased cookie sheet. Let stand until set. Store tightly covered at room temperature.

Makes about 3 dozen cookies

Quick Chocolate Softies

- 1 package (18.25 ounces) devil's food cake mix
- ⅓ cup water
- ¼ cup butter or margarine, softened
- 1 egg
- 1 cup white chocolate baking chips
- ½ cup coarsely chopped walnuts

Preheat oven to 350°F. Grease cookie sheets. Combine cake mix, water, butter and egg in large bowl. Beat with electric mixer at low speed until moistened. Increase speed to medium; beat 1 minute. (Dough will be thick.) Stir in chips and nuts; mix until well blended. Drop dough by heaping teaspoonfuls 2 inches apart onto prepared cookie sheets.

Bake 10 to 12 minutes or until set. Let cookies stand on cookie sheets 1 minute. Remove cookies to wire racks; cool completely.

Makes about 4 dozen cookies

BAKING SECRET

Grease cookie sheets only if directed to do so in the recipe. Some cookie doughs are high enough in fat that they will not stick to the sheet.

Bananaramas

- 1¼ cups firmly packed light brown sugar
- ¾ cup creamy peanut butter
- ½ CRISCO® Stick or ½ cup CRISCO® all-vegetable shortening
- 1 cup mashed banana
- 3 tablespoons milk
- 1½ teaspoons vanilla
- ½ teaspoon almond extract
- 1 egg
- 2 cups all-purpose flour
- ¾ teaspoon baking soda
- ¾ teaspoon salt
- 1½ cups milk chocolate chunks or semisweet chocolate chunks*
- 1 cup peanuts or coarsely chopped pecans (optional)

*A combination of milk chocolate and semisweet chocolate chunks can be used.

1. Heat oven to 350°F. Place sheets of foil on countertop for cooling cookies.

2. Place brown sugar, peanut butter, shortening, banana, milk, vanilla and almond extract in large bowl. Beat at medium speed of electric mixer until well blended. Add egg; beat just until blended.

3. Combine flour, baking soda and salt. Add to shortening mixture; beat at low speed just until blended. Stir in chocolate chunks and nuts, if desired.

4. Drop dough by rounded measuring tablespoonfuls 2 inches apart onto ungreased cookie sheets.

5. Bake one cookie sheet at a time at 350°F for 11 to 13 minutes or until cookies are light brown around edges. *Do not overbake.* Cool 2 minutes on cookie sheet. Remove cookies to foil to cool completely.

Makes about 4 dozen cookies

Quick Chocolate Softies

Chewy Oatmeal Cookies

1¼ cups firmly packed light brown sugar
¾ Butter Flavor CRISCO® Stick or ¾ cup Butter Flavor CRISCO® all-vegetable shortening
1 egg
⅓ cup milk
1½ teaspoons vanilla
3 cups quick oats, uncooked
1 cup all-purpose flour
½ teaspoon baking soda
½ teaspoon salt
¼ teaspoon cinnamon
1 cup raisins
1 cup coarsely chopped walnuts

1. Heat oven to 375°F. Grease cookie sheets. Place sheets of foil on countertop for cooling cookies.

2. Place brown sugar, shortening, egg, milk and vanilla in large bowl. Beat at medium speed of electric mixer until well blended.

3. Combine oats, flour, baking soda, salt and cinnamon. Add to shortening mixture; beat at low speed just until blended. Stir in raisins and walnuts.

4. Drop dough by rounded measuring tablespoonfuls 2 inches apart onto prepared cookie sheets.

5. Bake one cookie sheet at a time at 375°F for 10 to 12 minutes or until cookies are lightly browned. *Do not overbake.* Cool 2 minutes on baking sheet. Remove cookies to foil to cool completely.

Makes about 2½ dozen cookies

Nutty Clusters

4 squares (1 ounce each) unsweetened chocolate, divided
1 cup granulated sugar
½ cup plus 2 tablespoons butter or margarine, softened, divided
1 egg
⅓ cup buttermilk
1 teaspoon vanilla
1¾ cups all-purpose flour
½ teaspoon baking soda
1 cup mixed salted nuts, coarsely chopped
2 cups powdered sugar
2 to 3 tablespoons water

For cookies: **PREHEAT** oven to 400°F. Line cookie sheets with parchment paper or leave ungreased. Melt 2 squares chocolate in heavy small saucepan over very low heat. Remove from heat; let cool.

BEAT granulated sugar and ½ cup butter in large bowl with electric mixer until smooth. Beat in melted chocolate, egg, buttermilk and vanilla until light. Stir in flour and baking soda just until blended. Stir in nuts.

DROP teaspoonfuls of dough 2 inches apart onto prepared cookie sheets.

BAKE 8 to 10 minutes or until almost no imprint remains when touched. Immediately transfer cookies to wire rack.

Meanwhile, for icing, **MELT** remaining 2 squares chocolate and 2 tablespoons butter in small heavy saucepan over low heat, stirring until completely melted. Add powdered sugar and water, mixing until smooth. Frost cookies while still warm.

Makes about 4 dozen cookies

Chewy Oatmeal Cookies

Heartwarming Fruit Desserts

You'll find a great-tasting fruit dessert for every season in this chapter. Try a warm cinnamony baked apple on a crisp fall evening, a satisfying fruity bread pudding to top off a winter dinner, a luscious fresh strawberry shortcake to celebrate spring or a cool succulent berry cobbler to end a hot summer day.

Fresh Berry Cobbler Cake

- **1 pint fresh berries (blueberries, blackberries, raspberries and/or strawberries)**
- **1 cup all-purpose flour**
- **1¼ cups sugar, divided**
- **1 teaspoon baking powder**
- **¼ teaspoon salt**
- **3 tablespoons butter or margarine**
- **½ cup milk**
- **1 tablespoon cornstarch**
- **1 cup cold water**
- **Additional berries (optional)**

Preheat oven to 375°F. Place berries in 9-inch square baking pan; set aside. Combine flour, ½ cup sugar, baking powder and salt in large bowl. Cut in butter with pastry blender or two knives until coarse crumbs form. Stir in milk. Spoon over berries. Combine remaining ¾ cup sugar and cornstarch in small bowl. Stir in water until sugar mixture dissolves; pour over berry mixture. Bake 35 to 40 minutes or until lightly browned. Serve warm or cool completely. Garnish with additional berries, if desired. *Makes 6 servings*

Favorite recipe from **Bob Evans Farms®**

BAKING SECRET

Most cobblers and crisps are best served warm or at room temperature the day they are made. Leftovers should be covered and refrigerated.

Fresh Berry Cobbler Cake

Almond-Pear Strudel

- **5 to 6 cups thinly sliced crisp pears (about 5)**
- **1 tablespoon grated lemon peel**
- **1 tablespoon lemon juice**
- **⅓ cup plus 1 teaspoon sugar, divided**
- **2 teaspoons ground cinnamon**
- **1 teaspoon ground nutmeg**
- **6 sheets (¼ pound) phyllo dough**
- **4 tablespoons melted butter or margarine, divided**
- **½ teaspoon almond extract**
- **¾ cup slivered almonds, toasted, divided**
- **Powdered sugar (optional)**

1. Place sliced pears in large microwavable container. Stir in lemon peel and lemon juice. Microwave on HIGH 6 minutes or until tender; cool. Combine ⅓ cup sugar, cinnamon and nutmeg in small bowl. Cover pears and refrigerate.

2. Lay 2 sheets of plastic wrap on work surface to make 20-inch square. Place 1 phyllo sheet in middle of plastic wrap. (Cover remaining dough with damp kitchen towel to prevent drying.) Brush 1 teaspoon melted butter onto phyllo sheet. Place second phyllo sheet over first; brush with 1 teaspoon butter. Repeat layering with remaining sheets of phyllo.

3. Preheat oven to 400°F. Drain pear mixture; toss with sugar mixture and almond extract. Spread pear mixture evenly over phyllo leaving 3-inch strip on far long side. Sprinkle pear mixture with ½ cup toasted almonds. Brush strip with 2 teaspoons melted butter. Beginning at long side of phyllo opposite strip, roll up jelly-roll style, forming strudel. Place seam-side down onto buttered baking sheet. Brush top with 1 teaspoon butter. Bake 20 minutes or until golden. Brush with 1 teaspoon butter. Stir remaining ¼ cup almonds and 1 teaspoon sugar with remaining teaspoons butter; sprinkle on top of strudel. Bake 5 minutes more. Cool 10 minutes; sprinkle with powdered sugar, if desired. *Makes 8 servings*

Note: To make ahead, complete steps 1 and 2. Cover and refrigerate pears overnight. Cover sugar mixture and set aside. Cover phyllo and remaining butter; refrigerate overnight. To complete recipe, proceed with step 3, melting reserved butter before using.

Granny Smith Crisp

- **5 cups peeled, cored and sliced Granny Smith apples**
- **½ cup sugar**
- **1 teaspoon ground cinnamon**
- **Streusel Topping (recipe follows)**

Heat oven to 350°F. In large bowl, toss apples with sugar and cinnamon; spread apple mixture in 11×8-inch baking pan. Prepare Streusel Topping; spread evenly over apples. Bake 35 to 40 minutes or until apples are tender. *Makes 6 servings*

Streusel Topping: In medium bowl, combine ¾ cup all-purpose flour, ¼ cup granulated sugar and ¼ cup packed brown sugar. With pastry blender or 2 knives, cut in ½ cup (1 stick) butter until crumbly mixture is formed. Stir in ½ cup quick rolled oats.

Favorite recipe from **Washington Apple Commission**

Almond-Pear Strudel

Giant Strawberry Shortcake

2 quarts fresh ripe strawberries, hulled, divided
5 tablespoons sugar, divided
½ cup (2 ounces) shredded ALPINE LACE® American Flavor Pasteurized Process Cheese Product
2 cups all-purpose flour
1 tablespoon baking powder
1 tablespoon grated lime peel, divided
¾ teaspoon salt
½ teaspoon baking soda
¼ cup unsalted butter, at room temperature
¼ cup vegetable shortening
¾ cup buttermilk
¼ cup egg substitute or 1 large whole egg
¾ cup low fat vanilla yogurt
½ cup fat free sour cream

1. Preheat oven to 450°F. Butter 12-inch fluted tart pan with 1-inch side and removable bottom. Using food processor or blender, purée 1 cup berries and 2 tablespoons of the sugar; pour into serving bowl. Slice remaining berries and toss with purée. Cover; let stand at room temperature.

2. In food processor, process cheese until finely ground. Add flour, 1 tablespoon of the sugar, the baking powder, 2 teaspoons lime peel, salt and baking soda; process 15 seconds. Transfer to a large bowl. Using pastry cutter or 2 knives, cut in butter and shortening until mixture resembles coarse crumbs. In small bowl, whisk buttermilk and egg substitute (or whole egg) and add to flour mixture. Mix just until a soft dough forms. Turn dough onto lightly floured board; knead for about 30 seconds. Pat dough on bottom and side of pan and trim edges to stand 1 inch high. Bake for 11 minutes or just until lightly browned. Let cake cool in pan on rack for 5 minutes.

3. Meanwhile, in small bowl, blend yogurt and sour cream with the remaining 2 tablespoons of sugar and 1 teaspoon of lime peel; refrigerate. To serve, remove side, leaving cake on removable bottom of pan; place on platter. Top with berry mixture and some yogurt-cream. Serve with remaining yogurt-cream.

Makes 12 servings

BAKING SECRET

To reduce the risk of bacterial contamination of eggs, always keep them cold. If a recipe calls for room temperature eggs, let them sit on the counter for 30 minutes or place them in bowl of warm, not hot, water for 10 minutes; then use them immediately.

Giant Strawberry Shortcake

Blueberry Bread Pudding with Caramel Sauce

Blueberry Bread Pudding with Caramel Sauce

- 8 slices white bread, cubed
- 1 cup fresh or frozen blueberries
- 2 cups skim milk
- 1 cup EGG BEATERS® Healthy Egg Substitute
- ⅔ cup sugar
- 1 teaspoon vanilla extract
- ¼ teaspoon ground cinnamon
- Caramel Sauce (recipe follows)

Place bread cubes in bottom of lightly greased 8×8×2-inch baking pan. Sprinkle with blueberries; set aside.

In large bowl, combine milk, Egg Beaters, sugar, vanilla and cinnamon; pour over bread mixture. Set pan in larger pan filled with 1-inch depth hot water. Bake at 350°F for 1 hour or until knife inserted in center comes out clean. Serve warm with Caramel Sauce. *Makes 9 servings*

Prep time: 20 minutes
Cook time: 1 hour

CARAMEL SAUCE: In small saucepan, over low heat, heat ¼ cup skim milk and 14 vanilla caramels until caramels are melted, stirring frequently.

Walnut-Raisin Baked Apples

- 6 large baking apples, such as Rome Beauty
- 1 cup plus 2 tablespoons packed light brown sugar, divided
- 1 cup (4 ounces) shredded ALPINE LACE® American Flavor Pasteurized Process Cheese Product
- ¾ cup golden raisins
- ⅓ cup chopped California walnuts, toasted
- 1 teaspoon ground cinnamon
- 3 tablespoons fresh lemon juice
- 2 cups apple cider

1. Preheat the oven to 375°F. Spray a shallow baking dish with nonstick cooking spray.

2. Core the apples, cutting almost through, but not through, the bottoms of the apples, leaving about a 2-inch-wide cavity in the centers. Pare apples one third of the way down from the top stem end, then place upright in the baking dish. If necessary, cut a thin slice off the bottoms of the apples so they stand firm.

3. In a small bowl, toss together the 1 cup of brown sugar, the cheese, raisins, walnuts and cinnamon. Using a small spoon, stuff one sixth of the cheese mixture into the cavity of each apple, mounding it in the center. Drizzle the lemon juice over the apples. Pour the cider in the baking dish around the apples.

4. Bake the apples, uncovered, for 35 minutes, basting every 10 minutes with the cider. Sprinkle with the remaining 2 tablespoons sugar and bake 10 minutes more or until the apples can be pierced easily with a fork. To serve, transfer each apple to a serving dish and spoon some of the cider sauce over each serving.

Makes 6 servings

Fresh Nectarine-Pineapple Cobbler

- 1 DOLE® Fresh Pineapple
- 3 cups sliced ripe DOLE® Nectarines or Peaches
- ½ cup sugar
- 2 tablespoons all-purpose flour
- ½ teaspoon ground cinnamon
- 1 cup buttermilk baking mix
- ½ cup low-fat or nonfat milk

• **Twist** crown from pineapple. Cut pineapple in half lengthwise. Cover and refrigerate one half for another use. Cut remaining pineapple in half lengthwise. Remove fruit from shell; core and chop fruit.

• **Combine** pineapple, nectarines, sugar, flour and cinnamon in large bowl. Spoon into 8-inch square glass baking dish.

• **Stir** baking mix and milk in small bowl until baking mix is just moistened; pour over fruit.

• **Bake** at 400°F 40 to 45 minutes or until fruit is tender and crust is lightly browned.

Makes 8 servings

Prep time: 20 minutes
Bake time: 45 minutes

BAKING SECRET

To hasten ripening of fruit, such as peaches, nectarines, plums and pears, place them in a closed paper bag at room temperature for several days. Store ripe fruit in the refrigerator and use within a few days.

BAKING SECRET

For fruit desserts with the best flavor, use fully ripened fruit.

Berry Cobbler

- **1 pint fresh raspberries (2½ cups)***
- **1 pint fresh blueberries or strawberries, sliced (2½ cups)***
- **⅓ cup sugar**
- **2 tablespoons cornstarch**
- **1 cup all-purpose flour**
- **1 tablespoon sugar**
- **1½ teaspoons baking powder**
- **¼ teaspoon salt**
- **½ cup milk**
- **⅓ cup butter or margarine, melted**
- **¼ teaspoon ground nutmeg**

*One (16-ounce) bag frozen raspberries and one (16-ounce) bag frozen blueberries or strawberries may be substituted for fresh berries. Thaw berries, reserving juices. Increase cornstarch to 3 tablespoons.

Preheat oven to 375°F. Combine berries, ⅓ cup sugar and cornstarch in medium bowl; toss lightly to coat. Spoon into 1½-quart or 8-inch square baking dish. Combine flour, 1 tablespoon sugar, baking powder and salt in medium bowl. Add milk and butter; mix just until dry ingredients are moistened. Drop six heaping tablespoonfuls of batter evenly over berries; sprinkle with nutmeg. Bake 25 minutes or until topping is golden brown and fruit is bubbly. Cool on wire rack. Serve warm or at room temperature.

Makes 6 servings

Cherry-Chocolate Crumble

- **1½ cups graham cracker crumbs**
- **3 tablespoons sugar**
- **¼ cup Prune Purée (recipe follows) or prepared prune butter**
- **¼ cup semisweet miniature chocolate chips**
- **2 cans (20 ounces each) cherry pie filling**

Preheat oven to 375°F. In medium bowl, mix crumbs and sugar. Cut in prune purée with pastry blender until mixture resembles coarse crumbs. Mix in chocolate chips. Spread pie filling evenly in 8-inch square baking dish or pan; cover evenly with crumb mixture. Bake in center of oven about 20 minutes until cherries are bubbly and topping is lightly browned. Cool on wire rack 15 minutes. Serve warm, topped with fat-free vanilla frozen yogurt, if desired.

Makes 8 servings

Prune Purée: Combine 1⅓ cups (8 ounces) pitted prunes and 6 tablespoons hot water in container of food processor or blender. Pulse on and off until prunes are finely chopped and smooth. Store leftovers in covered container in refrigerator for up to two months. Makes 1 cup.

Favorite recipe from **California Prune Board**

Berry Cobbler

Streusel Topped Peach Cobbler

1 can (29 ounces) *or* 2 cans (16 ounces each) cling peach slices in syrup
⅓ cup plus 1 tablespoon granulated sugar, divided
1 tablespoon cornstarch
½ teaspoon vanilla
½ cup packed brown sugar
2 cups all-purpose flour, divided
⅓ cup uncooked quick oats
¼ cup margarine or butter, melted
½ teaspoon ground cinnamon
½ teaspoon salt
½ cup shortening
4 to 5 tablespoons cold water
Sweetened Whipped Cream (recipe follows)

Drain peach slices; reserve ¾ cup syrup. Combine ⅓ cup granulated sugar and cornstarch in small saucepan. Slowly add reserved syrup. Stir well. Cook over low heat, stirring constantly, until thickened. Add vanilla. Set aside.

Combine brown sugar, ½ cup flour, oats, margarine and cinnamon in small bowl; stir until mixture forms coarse crumbs. Set aside.

Preheat oven to 350°F. Combine remaining 1½ cups flour, 1 tablespoon granulated sugar and salt in small bowl. Cut in shortening until mixture forms pea-sized pieces. Sprinkle water, 1 tablespoon at a time, over flour mixture. Toss lightly with fork until mixture holds together. Press together to form a ball.

Press dough between hands to form a 5- to 6-inch disc. Roll dough into square, ⅛ inch thick, on lightly floured surface. Cut into 10-inch square. Press dough onto bottom and 1 inch up sides of 8-inch square baking dish.

Arrange peaches over crust. Pour sauce over peaches. Sprinkle with crumb topping. Bake 45 minutes. Prepare Sweetened Whipped Cream. Serve cobbler warm or at room temperature with Sweetened Whipped Cream.

Makes about 6 servings

Sweetened Whipped Cream

1 cup whipping cream, chilled
3 tablespoons sugar
½ teaspoon vanilla

Chill large bowl and beaters thoroughly. Pour chilled whipping cream into bowl and beat with electric mixer at high speed until soft peaks form. Gradually add sugar and vanilla. Whip until stiff peaks form.

Apple Crisp

5 cups peeled and sliced apples
½ cup raisins
1 cup all-purpose flour
½ cup sugar
½ teaspoon baking powder
½ teaspoon salt
1 egg
⅓ cup butter or margarine, melted
Ground cinnamon to taste
Vanilla ice cream (optional)

Preheat oven to 350°F. Combine apples and raisins in 8-inch square baking pan. Combine flour, sugar, baking powder and salt. Stir in egg with fork until crumbly. Sprinkle over apple mixture. Drizzle with butter and sprinkle with cinnamon. Bake 30 minutes or until lightly browned and apples are tender. Serve warm with vanilla ice cream, if desired. Refrigerate leftovers.

Makes 9 servings

Favorite recipe from **Bob Evans Farms®**

Streusel Topped Peach Cobbler

Country Breads

Warm breads on beautiful country mornings—what a wonderful memory! Even if you can't get to the country now, your family can enjoy cozy times at home in a kitchen filled with the aromas of freshly baked breads.

Orange-Currant Scones

1½ cups all-purpose flour
¼ cup plus 1 teaspoon sugar, divided
1 teaspoon baking powder
¼ teaspoon salt
¼ teaspoon baking soda
⅓ cup currants
1 tablespoon grated orange peel
6 tablespoons chilled butter or margarine, cut into small pieces
½ cup buttermilk, plain yogurt, or regular or nonfat sour cream

1. Preheat oven to 425°F.

2. Combine flour, ¼ cup sugar, baking powder, salt and baking soda in large bowl. Stir in currants and orange peel.

3. Cut in butter with pastry blender or 2 knives until mixture resembles coarse crumbs.

4. Stir in buttermilk. Stir until mixture forms soft dough that clings together. (Dough will be sticky.)

5. Lightly flour hands and shape dough into a ball. Pat dough into 8-inch round on lightly greased baking sheet. Cut dough into 8 wedges with floured chef's knife.

6. Sprinkle wedges with remaining 1 teaspoon sugar. Bake 18 to 20 minutes or until lightly browned.

Makes 8 scones

Orange-Currant Scones

BAKING SECRET

To test if a yeast dough has risen properly, lightly press two fingertips about one-half inch into the dough. The dough is ready if an indentation remains when fingertips are removed.

Cinnamon-Raisin Bread

- **1 package active dry yeast**
- **½ cup plus 1 teaspoon sugar, divided**
- **¼ cup warm water (105° to 115°F)**
- **2 eggs**
- **3 to 3½ cups all-purpose flour, divided**
- **1 teaspoon salt**
- **⅔ cup warm milk (105° to 115°F)**
- **3 tablespoons butter or margarine, softened**
- **1 teaspoon vanilla**
- **¾ cup raisins**
- **1 tablespoon ground cinnamon**
- **1 tablespoon butter or margarine, melted**
- **1 tablespoon water**

To proof yeast, sprinkle yeast and 1 teaspoon sugar over warm water in small bowl; stir until yeast is dissolved. Let stand 5 minutes or until mixture is bubbly. Separate 1 egg. Place yolk in another bowl; set aside. Cover white and reserve in refrigerator.

Combine 1½ cups flour, ¼ cup sugar and salt in large bowl. Gradually beat yeast mixture, warm milk and softened butter into flour mixture with electric mixer at low speed. Increase speed to medium; beat 2 minutes. Reduce speed to low. Beat in remaining whole egg, egg yolk and vanilla. Increase speed to medium; beat 2 minutes. Stir in raisins and enough additional flour, about 1½ cups, to make soft dough. Turn out dough onto lightly floured surface; flatten slightly. Knead dough about 5 minutes or until smooth and elastic, adding ½ cup more flour to prevent sticking, if necessary. (Dough will be soft and slightly sticky.)

Shape dough into ball; place in large greased bowl. Turn dough over so that top is greased. Cover with towel; let rise in warm place 1 to 1½ hours or until doubled in bulk. Punch down dough. Knead dough on lightly floured surface 1 minute. Cover with towel; let rest 10 minutes. Grease 9×5-inch loaf pan; set aside. Combine remaining ¼ cup sugar and cinnamon. Place 1 tablespoon mixture in small cup; reserve.

Roll dough into 20×9-inch rectangle with lightly floured rolling pin. Brush with 1 tablespoon melted butter. Sprinkle ¼ cup cinnamon mixture evenly over butter. Starting with 1 (9-inch) side, roll up dough jelly-roll fashion. Pinch ends and seam to seal. Place loaf, seam side down, in prepared pan, tucking ends under. Cover with towel; let rise in warm place about 1¼ hours or until doubled in bulk. (Dough should rise to top of pan.)

Preheat oven to 350°F. Combine reserved egg white and 1 tablespoon water in small bowl. Brush loaf with egg white mixture; sprinkle with reserved 1 tablespoon cinnamon mixture.

Bake 40 to 45 minutes or until loaf sounds hollow when tapped. Immediately remove from pan; cool completely on wire rack.

Makes 1 loaf

Cinnamon-Raisin Bread

Maple Nut Twist

1 recipe Sweet Yeast Dough (recipe follows)
2 tablespoons butter or margarine, melted
2 tablespoons honey
½ cup chopped pecans
¼ cup granulated sugar
2½ teaspoons maple extract, divided
½ teaspoon ground cinnamon
1 cup sifted powdered sugar
5 teaspoons milk

Prepare Sweet Yeast Dough; let rise as directed. Combine butter and honey in custard cup; set aside. Combine pecans, granulated sugar, 2 teaspoons maple extract and cinnamon in small bowl. Toss to coat; set aside.

Grease 2 baking sheets; set aside. Cut dough in half; cut half of dough into 2 pieces. Roll out 1 piece dough into 9-inch circle on lightly floured surface with lightly floured rolling pin. (Keep remaining dough covered with towel.) Place on prepared baking sheet. Brush half of butter mixture over dough. Sprinkle half of pecan mixture over butter.

Roll remaining piece dough into 9-inch circle. Carefully place dough over pecan filling, stretching dough as necessary to cover. Pinch edges to seal. Place 1-inch biscuit cutter* in center of circle as cutting guide, being careful not to cut through dough. Cut dough into 12 wedges with scissors or sharp knife, from edge of circle to edge of biscuit cutter, cutting through all layers. Pick up wide edge of 1 wedge, twist several times and lay back down on prepared sheet. Repeat twisting procedure with remaining 11 wedges. Repeat with remaining half of dough, butter mixture and pecan mixture. Cover coffee cakes with towel. Let rise in warm place about 1 hour or until doubled in bulk.

Preheat oven to 350°F. Bake on 2 racks in oven 20 to 25 minutes or until coffee cakes are golden brown and sound hollow when tapped. (Rotate baking sheets top to bottom halfway through baking.) Immediately remove from baking sheets; cool on wire racks about 30 minutes.

Combine powdered sugar, milk and remaining ½ teaspoon maple extract in small bowl until smooth. Drizzle over warm coffee cakes.

Makes 24 servings (2 coffee cakes)

*Or, use the lid of an herb jar if biscuit cutter is not available.

Sweet Yeast Dough

4 to 4¼ cups all-purpose flour, divided
½ cup sugar
2 packages active dry yeast
1 teaspoon salt
¾ cup milk
4 tablespoons butter or margarine
2 eggs
1 teaspoon vanilla

Combine 1 cup flour, sugar, yeast and salt in large bowl; set aside.

Combine milk and butter in 1-quart saucepan. Heat over low heat until mixture is 120° to 130°F. (Butter does not need to completely melt.) Gradually beat milk mixture into flour mixture with electric mixer at low speed. Increase speed to medium; beat 2 minutes. Reduce speed to low. Beat in eggs, vanilla and 1 cup flour. Increase speed to medium; beat 2 minutes. Stir in enough additional flour, about 2 cups, to make soft dough.

Turn out dough onto lightly floured surface; flatten slightly. Knead dough about 5 minutes or until smooth and elastic, adding ¼ cup more flour to prevent sticking if necessary. Shape dough into a ball; place in large greased bowl. Turn dough over so that top is greased. Cover with towel; let rise in warm place 1½ to 2 hours or until doubled in bulk. Punch down dough. Knead dough on lightly floured surface 1 minute. Cover with towel; let rest 10 minutes.

REFRIGERATOR SWEET YEAST DOUGH: Prepare Sweet Yeast Dough. Shape dough into a ball; place in large greased bowl. Turn dough over so that top is greased. Cover with plastic wrap; refrigerate 3 to 24 hours. Punch down dough. Knead dough on lightly floured surface 1 to 2 minutes. Cover with towel; let dough rest 20 minutes before shaping and second rising. (Second rising may take up to 1½ hours.)

Maple Nut Twist

BAKING SECRET

Use large eggs for all recipes unless the ingredient list indicates another size.

Cinnamon Honey Buns

- **¼ cup butter or margarine, softened and divided**
- **½ cup honey, divided**
- **¼ cup chopped toasted nuts**
- **2 teaspoons ground cinnamon**
- **1 loaf (1 pound) frozen bread dough, thawed according to package directions**
- **⅔ cup raisins**

Grease 12 muffin cups with 1 tablespoon butter. To prepare honey-nut topping, mix together 1 tablespoon butter, ¼ cup honey and chopped nuts. Place 1 teaspoon topping in each muffin cup.

To prepare filling, mix together remaining 2 tablespoons butter, remaining ¼ cup honey and cinnamon. Roll out bread dough onto floured surface into 18×8-inch rectangle. Spread filling evenly over dough. Sprinkle evenly with raisins. Starting with long side, roll dough into log. Cut log into 12 (1½-inch) slices. Place 1 slice, cut-side up, into each prepared muffin cup. Set muffin pan in warm place; let dough rise 30 minutes.

Place muffin pan on foil-lined baking sheet. Bake at 375°F 20 minutes or until buns are golden brown. Remove from oven; cool in pan 5 minutes. Invert muffin pan to remove buns. *Makes 12 buns*

Favorite recipe from **National Honey Board**

Southwestern Biscuits

- **2¼ cups all-purpose flour**
- **2 tablespoons granulated sugar**
- **1 tablespoon baking powder**
- **3 tablespoons butter or margarine, softened**
- **1 cup (8-ounce can) cream-style corn**
- **½ cup (4-ounce can) ORTEGA® Diced Green Chiles**
- **1 egg, slightly beaten**
- **1 tablespoon chopped fresh cilantro (optional)**

COMBINE flour, sugar and baking powder in large bowl. Cut in butter with pastry blender or two knives until mixture resembles coarse crumbs.

STIR in corn, chiles, egg and cilantro; combine just until mixture holds together. Knead dough 10 times on well-floured surface. Pat dough into ¾-inch thickness. Cut into 3-inch biscuits. Place on greased baking sheets.

BAKE in preheated 400°F. oven for 20 to 25 minutes or until wooden pick inserted in center comes out clean. Let stand for 5 minutes; remove to wire racks to cool completely. *Makes 8 biscuits*

Tip: Serve these delicious biscuits with jalapeño butter. To make this spread with a kick, blend 1 to 2 teaspoons ORTEGA® Diced Jalapeños into ½ cup (1 stick) softened butter.

Cinnamon Honey Buns

BAKING SECRET

Mix muffins just until the dry ingredients are moistened; some lumps may remain. Overmixing will give muffins a tough texture.

Green Onion Cream Cheese Breakfast Biscuits

- **2 cups all-purpose flour**
- **1 tablespoon baking powder**
- **1 tablespoon sugar**
- **¾ teaspoon salt**
- **1 package (3 ounces) cream cheese**
- **¼ cup vegetable shortening**
- **½ cup finely chopped green onions**
- **⅔ cup milk**

1. Preheat oven to 450°F.

2. Combine flour, baking powder, sugar and salt in medium bowl. Cut in cream cheese and shortening with pastry blender or 2 knives until mixture resembles coarse crumbs. Stir in green onions.

3. Make well in center of flour mixture. Add milk; stir until mixture forms soft dough that clings together and forms a ball.

4. Turn out dough onto well-floured surface. Knead dough gently 10 to 12 times. Roll or pat dough to ½-inch thickness. Cut out dough with floured 3-inch biscuit cutter.

5. Place biscuits 2 inches apart on *ungreased* large baking sheet. Bake 10 to 12 minutes or until tops and bottoms are golden brown. Serve warm.

Makes 8 biscuits

Carrot Pecan Muffins

- **1¾ cups all-purpose flour**
- **1 teaspoon baking soda**
- **1 teaspoon ground cinnamon**
- **¼ teaspoon ground nutmeg**
- **1 cup sweetened applesauce**
- **½ cup firmly packed light brown sugar**
- **⅓ cup FLEISCHMANN'S® 70% Corn Oil Spread, melted**
- **¼ cup EGG BEATERS® Healthy Egg Substitute**
- **1 cup shredded carrots**
- **½ cup pecan halves, chopped, divided**
- **Powdered Sugar Glaze (recipe follows)**

In small bowl, combine flour, baking soda, cinnamon and nutmeg; set aside.

In large bowl, combine applesauce, brown sugar, spread and Egg Beaters. Stir in flour mixture, carrots and ⅓ cup pecans just until moistened. Spoon batter into 12 lightly greased 2½-inch muffin-pan cups. Bake at 350°F for 20 to 25 minutes or until lightly browned. Cool on wire rack. Drizzle tops of muffins with Powdered Sugar Glaze; sprinkle with remaining pecans. *Makes 1 dozen muffins*

Prep time: 25 minutes
Cook time: 25 minutes

POWDERED SUGAR GLAZE: In small bowl, combine 1 cup powdered sugar and 5 to 6 teaspoons water until smooth.

Green Onion Cream Cheese Breakfast Biscuits

Lemon Poppy Seed Muffins

Lemon Poppy Seed Muffins

- **3 cups all-purpose flour**
- **1 cup sugar**
- **3 tablespoons poppy seeds**
- **1 tablespoon grated lemon peel**
- **2 teaspoons baking powder**
- **1 teaspoon baking soda**
- **½ teaspoon salt**
- **1 container (16 ounces) plain low-fat yogurt**
- **½ cup fresh lemon juice**
- **¼ cup vegetable oil**
- **2 eggs, beaten**
- **1½ teaspoons vanilla**

Preheat oven to 400°F. Grease 12 (3½-inch) large muffin cups; set aside.

Combine flour, sugar, poppy seeds, lemon peel, baking powder, baking soda and salt in large bowl. Combine yogurt, lemon juice, oil, eggs and vanilla in small bowl until well blended. Stir into flour mixture just until moistened. Spoon into prepared muffin cups, filling two-thirds full.

Bake 25 to 30 minutes or until wooden pick inserted in center comes out clean. Cool in pans on wire racks 5 minutes. Remove from pans. Cool on wire racks 10 minutes. Serve warm or cool completely. *Makes 12 jumbo muffins*

Cheese & Herb Biscuits

- **4 cups all-purpose flour**
- **2 tablespoons sugar**
- **2 tablespoons baking powder**
- **1 teaspoon salt**
- **11 tablespoons butter or margarine, cold**
- **1¼ cups milk, cold**
- **Additional all-purpose flour**
- **1 cup (4 ounces) shredded Cheddar cheese**
- **½ cup chopped parsley or other fresh herbs**

Preheat oven to 425°F. Combine first 4 ingredients in large bowl. Cut butter into ¼-inch-thick chunks; add to flour mixture. Cut in butter with pastry blender or two knives until butter is broken into pea-size pieces. Make well in flour mixture; pour milk into well. Gently toss together with fork *just* until blended. *Do not overwork dough.*

Turn dough onto lightly floured work surface. To knead dough, gently pat or roll into ½-inch-thick rectangle; fold in half, adding more flour to work surface as needed to prevent sticking. Turn dough a ¼ turn. Repeat kneading at least 5 times, then sprinkle dough with cheese and herbs. Continue kneading dough until it is holds together and forms a soft dough.

Roll out dough to ½-inch thickness; cut out biscuits with 2-inch biscuit cutter. Place on lightly greased baking sheet, about ½ inch apart. Bake 15 to 20 minutes or until lightly browned. Cool slightly before removing from baking sheets. Serve warm.

Makes about 24 biscuits

Tip: Wrap leftover biscuits in foil and freeze. Reheat in foil in 325°F oven 10 minutes.

Serving suggestion: Brush tops with melted butter when removed from oven for an even more tender crust.

Favorite recipe from **Bob Evans Farms®**

Fiesta Corn Bread

- **2¼ cups all-purpose flour**
- **1¾ cups ALBERS® Yellow Corn Meal**
- **1½ cups (6 ounces) shredded Cheddar cheese**
- **1 cup (7-ounce can) ORTEGA® Diced Green Chiles**
- **½ cup granulated sugar**
- **2 tablespoons baking powder**
- **1½ teaspoons salt**
- **2 cups milk**
- **⅔ cup vegetable oil**
- **2 eggs, lightly beaten**

COMBINE flour, cornmeal, cheese, chiles, sugar, baking powder and salt in large bowl. Add milk, oil and eggs; stir just until moistened. Spread into greased 13×9-inch baking pan.

BAKE in preheated 375°F. oven for 30 to 35 minutes or until wooden pick inserted in center comes out clean. Cool in pan on wire rack for 10 minutes before serving.

Makes 20 servings

BAKING SECRET

Knead biscuit dough lightly (10 to 12 times) to bring it together for shaping. Too much kneading will make biscuits tough and mealy.

Coffee Walnut Chocolate Chip Muffins

- **½ cup (1 stick) butter or margarine, softened**
- **½ cup granulated sugar**
- **½ cup packed light brown sugar**
- **2 to 3 tablespoons powdered instant coffee**
- **2 teaspoons vanilla extract**
- **1¾ cups all-purpose flour**
- **1 tablespoon baking powder**
- **½ teaspoon salt**
- **2 eggs**
- **⅔ cup milk**
- **1½ cups coarsely chopped walnuts**
- **¾ cup HERSHEY'S® Semi-Sweet Chocolate Chips**

Heat oven to 350°F. Line twelve muffin cups (2½ inches in diameter) with paper bake cups. In large bowl, beat butter, granulated sugar, brown sugar, coffee and vanilla until creamy. Stir together flour, baking powder and salt. Beat together eggs and milk; add alternately with flour mixture to butter mixture, stirring just to combine. Stir in walnuts and chocolate chips. Fill muffin cups half full with batter. Bake 20 to 25 minutes. Cool 5 minutes; remove from pans to wire rack. Cool completely. *Makes 12 muffins*

Favorite Corn Muffins

- **1 cup all-purpose flour**
- **¾ cup cornmeal**
- **¼ cup bran**
- **2 teaspoons baking powder**
- **1½ teaspoons salt**
- **½ teaspoon baking soda**
- **1 cup dairy sour cream**
- **2 eggs**
- **¼ cup honey**
- **¼ cup (½ stick) butter, melted**

Preheat oven to 425°F. Coat 12-cup muffin pan generously with butter. Combine flour, cornmeal, bran, baking powder, salt and baking soda in large bowl. Beat sour cream, eggs, honey and butter in medium bowl until well blended. Add sour cream mixture to flour mixture; stir just until dry ingredients are evenly moistened. Spoon batter into prepared muffin cups. Bake 15 to 20 minutes. Cool in pan 5 minutes before removing. Serve warm.

Makes 12 muffins

Favorite recipe from **Wisconsin Milk Marketing Board**

Honey Zucchini Bread

- **1 egg**
- **¾ cup honey**
- **3 tablespoons vegetable oil**
- **1 teaspoon vanilla**
- **2½ cups all-purpose flour**
- **1½ teaspoons baking powder**
- **1 teaspoon grated orange peel**
- **½ teaspoon baking soda**
- **½ teaspoon ground ginger**
- **¼ teaspoon salt**
- **1½ cups grated zucchini**
- **½ cup sunflower seeds**

Beat egg slightly in large bowl. Add honey, oil and vanilla; mix well. Combine flour, baking powder, orange peel, baking soda, ginger and salt in medium bowl. Add flour mixture, zucchini and sunflower seeds to honey mixture; mix until well blended. Spoon batter into well greased 9×5×3-inch loaf pan. Bake at 325°F about 1 hour or until wooden pick inserted near center comes out clean. Cool 10 minutes in pan; remove from pan and cool completely.

Makes 12 servings

Favorite recipe from **National Honey Board**

Duncan Hines®

BAKE IT *Easy*

CONTENTS

BUSY-DAY BROWNIES, BARS & COOKIES

PRALINE BROWNIES

BROWNIES

1 package Duncan Hines® Milk Chocolate Chunk Brownie Mix
2 eggs
⅓ cup water
⅓ cup Crisco® Vegetable Oil
¾ cup chopped pecans

TOPPING

¾ cup firmly packed brown sugar
¾ cup chopped pecans
¼ cup butter or margarine, melted
2 tablespoons milk
½ teaspoon vanilla extract

1 Preheat oven to 350°F. Grease bottom of 9-inch square pan.

2 **For brownies,** combine brownie mix, eggs, water, oil and ¾ cup pecans in large bowl. Stir with spoon until well blended, about 50 strokes. Spread in pan. Bake at 350°F 35 to 40 minutes. Remove from oven.

3 **For topping,** combine brown sugar, ¾ cup pecans, melted butter, milk and vanilla extract in small bowl. Stir with spoon until well blended. Spread over hot brownies. Return to oven. Bake 15 minutes or until topping is set. Cool completely. Cut into bars. *16 brownies*

Tip: To keep leftover pecans fresh, store in freezer in airtight container.

PRALINE BROWNIES

DOUBLE "TOPPED" BROWNIES

BROWNIES

- **1 package Duncan Hines® Double Fudge Brownie Mix**
- **2 eggs**
- **⅓ cup water**
- **¼ cup Crisco® Vegetable Oil**
- **½ cup flaked coconut**
- **½ cup chopped nuts**

FROSTING

- **3 cups confectioners sugar**
- **⅓ cup butter or margarine, softened**
- **1½ teaspoons vanilla extract**
- **2 to 3 tablespoons milk**

TOPPING

- **3 squares (3 ounces) unsweetened chocolate**
- **1 tablespoon butter or margarine**

1 Preheat oven to 350°F. Grease bottom of 13×9×2-inch pan.

2 **For brownies,** combine brownie mix, fudge packet from Mix, eggs, water and oil in large bowl. Stir with spoon until well blended, about 50 strokes. Stir in coconut and nuts. Spread in pan. Bake at 350°F 27 to 30 minutes or until set. Cool completely.

3 **For frosting,** combine confectioners sugar, ⅓ cup butter and vanilla extract. Stir in milk, 1 tablespoon at a time, until frosting is of spreading consistency. Spread over brownies. Refrigerate until frosting is firm, about 30 minutes.

4 **For topping,** melt chocolate and 1 tablespoon butter in small bowl over hot water; stir until smooth. Drizzle over frosting. Refrigerate until chocolate is firm, about 15 minutes. Cut into bars.

48 brownies

Tip: Chocolate topping can be prepared in microwave oven. Place chocolate and butter in microwave-safe bowl and microwave at MEDIUM (50% power) 2 to 2½ minutes; stir until smooth.

TRIPLE CHOCOLATE COOKIES

1 package Duncan Hines® Moist Deluxe® Swiss Chocolate Cake Mix
½ cup butter or margarine, melted
1 egg
½ cup semi-sweet chocolate chips
½ cup milk chocolate chips
½ cup coarsely chopped white chocolate
½ cup chopped pecans

1 Preheat oven to 375°F.

2 Combine cake mix, melted butter and egg in large bowl. Beat at low speed with electric mixer until blended. Stir in all 3 chocolates and pecans.

3 Drop by rounded tablespoonfuls onto ungreased baking sheets. Bake at 375°F 9 to 11 minutes. Cool 1 minute on baking sheet. Remove to cooling racks.

3½ to 4 dozen cookies

Tip: Cookies may be stored in an airtight container in freezer for up to 6 months.

BUTTERSCOTCH SPICE COOKIES

1 package Duncan Hines® Moist Deluxe® Spice Cake Mix
2 eggs
½ cup Crisco® Vegetable Oil
1 teaspoon vanilla extract
1 cup butterscotch chips

1 Preheat oven to 375°F.

2 Combine cake mix, eggs, oil and vanilla extract in large bowl. Beat at low speed with electric mixer until blended. Stir in butterscotch chips. Drop by rounded teaspoonfuls 2 inches apart onto ungreased baking sheets. Bake at 375°F 8 to 10 minutes or until set. Cool 2 minutes on baking sheets. Remove to cooling racks. Cool completely. Store in airtight container.

3 dozen cookies

Tip: For chewy cookies, bake for 8 minutes. Cookies will be slightly puffed when removed from the oven and will settle while cooling.

EASY MINT BROWNIES

1 package Duncan Hines® Walnut Brownie Mix
4 bars (5.3 ounces each) cookies and mint chocolate candy bars
⅓ cup chopped walnuts, for garnish (optional)

1 Preheat oven to 350°F. Grease bottom of 13×9×2-inch pan.

2 Prepare and bake brownies following package directions for basic recipe chewy brownies. Break chocolate candy bars along scored lines. Place pieces immediately on hot brownies. Cover pan with aluminum foil for 3 to 5 minutes or until chocolate is shiny and soft. Spread gently to cover surface of brownies. Sprinkle with chopped walnuts, if desired. Cool completely. Cut into bars. *18 brownies*

Tip: Always use the pan size called for in Duncan Hines® recipes. Using a different size can give the brownies an altogether different texture.

CANDY BAR BROWNIES

1 package Duncan Hines® Chewy Fudge Brownie Mix (19.8 ounces)
4 bars (5.3 ounces each) milk chocolate candy bars
⅓ cup mini candy-coated milk chocolate pieces

1 Preheat oven to 350°F. Grease bottom of 13×9×2-inch pan.

2 Prepare and bake brownies following package directions for basic recipe chewy brownies. Break chocolate candy bars along scored lines. Place pieces immediately on hot brownies. Cover pan with aluminum foil for 3 to 5 minutes or until chocolate is shiny and soft. Spread gently to cover surface of brownies. Sprinkle with candy-coated chocolate pieces. Cool completely. Cut into bars. *18 brownies*

Tip: For another delicious candy topping, try sprinkling melted chocolate with ½ cup chopped chocolate-covered toffee chips.

WHITE CHOCOLATE BROWNIES

- 1 package Duncan Hines® Milk Chocolate Chunk Brownie Mix
- 2 eggs
- ⅓ cup water
- ⅓ cup Crisco® Vegetable Oil
- ¾ cup coarsely chopped white chocolate
- ¼ cup sliced almonds

1 Preheat oven to 350°F. Grease bottom of 13×9×2-inch pan.

2 Combine brownie mix, eggs, water and oil in large bowl. Stir with spoon until well blended, about 50 strokes. Stir in white chocolate. Spread in pan. Sprinkle top with almonds. Bake at 350°F 25 to 28 minutes or until set. Cool completely. Cut into bars. *48 small or 24 large brownies*

Tip: For decadent brownies, combine 2 ounces coarsely chopped white chocolate and 2 teaspoons Crisco® Shortening in small heavy saucepan. Melt on low heat, stirring constantly. Drizzle over brownies.

CINDY'S FUDGY BROWNIES

- 1 package Duncan Hines® Chewy Fudge Brownie Mix (19.8 ounces)
- 1 egg
- ⅓ cup water
- ⅓ cup Crisco® Vegetable Oil
- ¾ cup semi-sweet chocolate chips
- ½ cup chopped pecans

1 Preheat oven to 350°F. Grease bottom of 13×9×2-inch pan.

2 Combine brownie mix, egg, water and oil in large bowl. Stir with spoon until well blended, about 50 strokes. Stir in chocolate chips. Spread in pan. Sprinkle with pecans. Bake at 350°F 25 to 28 minutes or until set. Cool completely. Cut into bars. *24 brownies*

Tip: Overbaking brownies will cause them to become dry. Follow the recommended baking times given in recipes closely.

WHITE CHOCOLATE BROWNIES

CHOCOLATE OAT CHEWIES

- 1 package Duncan Hines® Moist Deluxe® Devil's Food Cake Mix
- 1⅓ cups old-fashioned oats
- 1 cup flaked coconut, toasted and divided
- ¾ cup butter or margarine, melted
- 2 eggs, beaten
- 1 teaspoon vanilla extract
- 5 bars (1.55 ounces each) milk chocolate, cut into rectangles

1 Preheat oven to 350°F.

2 Combine cake mix, oats, ½ cup coconut, melted butter, eggs and vanilla extract in large bowl. Beat at low speed with electric mixer until blended. Cover and chill 15 minutes.

3 Shape dough into 1-inch balls. Place balls 2 inches apart on ungreased baking sheet. Bake at 350°F 12 minutes or until tops are slightly cracked. Remove from oven. Press one milk chocolate rectangle into center of each cookie. Sprinkle with remaining ½ cup coconut. Remove to cooling racks. Cool completely. Store in airtight container. *4½ dozen cookies*

Tip: To toast coconut, spread on cookie sheet and bake at 350°F for 3 minutes. Stir and bake 1 to 2 minutes longer or until light golden brown.

CHOCOLATE CHIP COOKIES

- 1 package Duncan Hines® Chocolate Chip Cookie Mix
- 1 egg
- 1 tablespoon water
- ⅓ cup MOTT'S® Natural Apple Sauce

1 Preheat oven to 375°F. Lightly grease baking sheet.

2 Follow instructions on box for MAKE DOUGH. Drop by measuring tablespoonfuls 2 inches apart onto greased baking sheets. Bake at 375°F 8 to 9 minutes. Cool 1 minute on baking sheet. Remove to cooling racks. *4 dozen cookies*

Note: "Get it All" cookies will have a more cake-like texture than cookies made from Basic Recipe.

CHOCOLATE OAT CHEWIES

BUTTER FUDGE FINGERS

1 package Duncan Hines® Chewy Fudge Brownie Mix (19.8 ounces)
1 container Duncan Hines® Creamy Homestyle Vanilla Buttercream Frosting
¼ cup semi-sweet chocolate chips
½ tablespoon Crisco® Shortening

1 Preheat oven to 350°F. Grease bottom of 13×9×2-inch pan.

2 Prepare, bake and cool brownies following package directions for basic recipe chewy brownies. Spread with Buttercream frosting.

3 Place chocolate chips and shortening in small resealable plastic bag; seal. Microwave at HIGH (100% power) 30 seconds, adding 15 to 30 seconds more if needed. Knead until blended. Snip pinpoint hole in corner of bag. Drizzle chocolate over frosting. Allow chocolate to set before cutting into bars. *18 brownies*

Tip: Another method for melting the chocolate and shortening in the sealed bag is to place it in a bowl of hot water for several minutes. Dry bag with paper towel. Knead, snip and pipe as directed above.

CINNAMON CRINKLES

2 tablespoons sugar
½ teaspoon ground cinnamon
2 eggs, separated
1 teaspoon water
¾ cup butter or margarine, softened
1 teaspoon vanilla extract
1 package Duncan Hines® Moist Deluxe® French Vanilla Cake Mix
48 whole almonds or pecan halves, for garnish

1 Preheat oven to 375°F. Combine sugar and cinnamon in small bowl. Set aside. Combine egg whites and water in another small bowl; beat lightly with fork. Set aside.

2 Combine butter, egg yolks and vanilla extract in large bowl. Blend in cake mix gradually. Beat at low speed with electric mixer until blended. Roll 1 rounded teaspoon of dough into ball. Dip half the ball into egg white mixture then into cinnamon-sugar mixture. Place ball sugar side up on ungreased baking sheet. Press nut on top. Repeat with remaining dough, placing balls 2 inches apart.

3 Bake at 375°F 9 to 12 minutes or until edges are light golden brown. Cool 2 minutes on baking sheets. Remove to cooling racks. Store in airtight container. *48 cookies*

Tip: Cookies will be slightly puffed when removed from the oven and will settle during cooling.

TOFFEE CRUNCH FANTASY

1 package Duncan Hines® Dark 'n Chunky Brownie Mix
2 eggs
⅓ cup water
⅓ cup Crisco® Vegetable Oil
2½ cups frozen non-dairy whipped topping, thawed
⅔ cup toffee chips, divided (see Tip)

1 Preheat oven to 350°F. Grease bottom of 9-inch round cake pan.

2 Combine brownie mix, eggs, water and oil in large bowl. Stir with spoon until well blended, about 50 strokes. Spread in pan. Bake at 350°F 35 to 40 minutes or until set. Cool completely.

3 Combine whipped topping and ½ cup toffee chips in large bowl. Spread on top of brownies. Garnish with remaining toffee chips. Refrigerate until ready to serve. Cut into wedges. *12 to 16 servings*

Tip: Coarsely chop several chocolate-covered toffee candy bars to prepare toffee chips, if ready-made toffee chips are not available.

CANDY DANDY BROWNIES

BROWNIES

1 package Duncan Hines® Chewy Fudge Brownie Mix (19.8 ounces)
1 egg
⅓ cup water
⅓ cup Crisco® Vegetable Oil

TOPPING

⅓ cup sugar
⅓ cup light corn syrup
⅓ cup Jif® Creamy Peanut Butter

FROSTING

½ cup semi-sweet chocolate chips
2 tablespoons butter or margarine
1 tablespoon light corn syrup
¼ cup sliced almonds, for garnish

1 Preheat oven to 350°F. Grease bottom of 13×9×2-inch pan.

2 **For brownies,** combine brownie mix, egg, water and oil in large bowl. Stir with spoon until well blended, about 50 strokes. Spread in pan. Bake at 350°F 25 to 28 minutes or until set. Cool in pan while preparing topping.

3 **For topping,** combine sugar and ⅓ cup corn syrup in heavy saucepan. Bring to boil on medium heat. Stir in peanut butter. Spread over warm brownies. Cool 10 to 15 minutes.

4 **For frosting,** combine chocolate chips, butter and 1 tablespoon corn syrup in pan. Cook, stirring constantly, on low heat until melted. Spread frosting over peanut butter layer. Sprinkle with almonds. Cool completely. Refrigerate until chocolate is firm, about 15 minutes. Cut into bars. *24 bars*

Tip: Always mix brownies by hand. Never use an electric mixer.

RICH 'N' CREAMY BROWNIE BARS

BROWNIES

- **1 package Duncan Hines® Double Fudge Brownie Mix**
- **2 eggs**
- **⅓ cup water**
- **¼ cup Crisco® Vegetable Oil**
- **½ cup chopped pecans**

TOPPING

- **1 package (8 ounces) cream cheese, softened**
- **2 eggs**
- **1 pound (3½ cups) confectioners sugar**
- **1 teaspoon vanilla extract**

1 Preheat oven to 350°F. Grease bottom of 13×9×2-inch pan.

2 **For brownies,** combine brownie mix, fudge packet from Mix, 2 eggs, water and oil in large bowl. Stir with spoon until well blended, about 50 strokes. Stir in pecans. Spread evenly in pan.

3 **For topping,** beat cream cheese in large bowl at medium speed with electric mixer until smooth. Beat in 2 eggs, confectioners sugar and vanilla extract until smooth. Spread evenly over brownie mixture. Bake at 350°F 45 to 50 minutes or until edges and top are golden brown and shiny. Cool completely. Refrigerate until well chilled. Cut into bars.

48 bars

Tip: To soften cream cheese quickly, unwrap and place in microwave-safe bowl. Microwave at HIGH (100% power) 15 seconds; add 10 to 15 seconds, if needed.

DOUBLE CHOCOLATE CHEWIES

- 1 package Duncan Hines® Moist Deluxe® Butter Recipe Fudge Cake Mix
- 2 eggs
- ½ cup butter or margarine, melted
- 1 package (6 ounces) semi-sweet chocolate chips
- 1 cup chopped nuts
- Confectioners sugar (optional)

1 Preheat oven to 350°F. Grease 13×9×2-inch pan.

2 Combine cake mix, eggs and melted butter in large bowl. Stir until thoroughly blended. (Mixture will be stiff.) Stir in chocolate chips and nuts. Press mixture evenly into greased pan. Bake at 350°F 25 to 30 minutes or until toothpick inserted in center comes out clean. DO NOT OVERBAKE. Cool completely. Cut into bars. Dust with confectioners sugar, if desired.

36 bars

Tip: For a special effect, cut paper towel into ¼-inch wide strips. Place strips in diagonal pattern on top of cooled bars before cutting. Place confectioners sugar in small strainer. Tap strainer lightly to dust surface with sugar. Carefully remove strips.

TOFFEE BROWNIE BARS

CRUST

- ¾ cup butter or margarine, softened
- ¾ cup firmly packed brown sugar
- 1 egg yolk
- ¾ teaspoon vanilla extract
- 1½ cups all-purpose flour

FILLING

- 1 package Duncan Hines® Chewy Fudge Brownie Mix (19.8 ounces)
- 1 egg
- ⅓ cup water
- ⅓ cup Crisco® Vegetable Oil

TOPPING

- 1 package (12 ounces) milk chocolate chips, melted
- ¾ cup finely chopped pecans

1 Preheat oven to 350°F. Grease 15½×10½×1-inch pan.

2 **For crust,** combine butter, brown sugar, egg yolk and vanilla extract in large bowl. Stir in flour. Spread in pan. Bake 15 minutes or until golden.

3 **For filling,** prepare brownie mix following package directions. Spread over hot crust. Bake 15 minutes or until surface appears set. Cool 30 minutes.

4 **For topping,** spread melted chocolate on top of brownie layer; sprinkle with pecans. Cool completely. *48 bars*

Tip: Bars may be made ahead and frozen in an airtight container for several weeks.

FESTIVE CHOCOLATE CHIP COOKIES

1 package Duncan Hines® Moist Deluxe® White Cake Mix
¼ cup firmly packed light brown sugar
1 egg
¾ cup Crisco® Vegetable Oil
1 package (6 ounces) semi-sweet chocolate chips
½ cup chopped pecans or walnuts
Assorted decors

1 Preheat oven to 350°F.

2 Combine cake mix, brown sugar, egg and oil in large bowl. Beat at low speed with electric mixer until blended. Stir in chocolate chips and pecans. Form dough into 1½-inch ball. Dip top of ball in decors. Place ball decor-side up on ungreased baking sheets. Repeat with remaining dough placing balls 2 inches apart on baking sheets. Bake at 350°F 10 to 12 minutes or until light golden brown around edges. Cool 2 minutes on baking sheets. Remove to cooling racks. Cool completely. Store in airtight container. *3 to 3½ dozen cookies*

Tip: Cool baking sheet completely before baking each batch of cookies.

COCONUT CLOUDS

2⅔ cups flaked coconut, divided
1 package Duncan Hines® Moist Deluxe® Yellow Cake Mix
1 egg
½ cup Crisco® Vegetable Oil
¼ cup water
1 teaspoon almond extract

1 Preheat oven to 350°F. Place 1⅓ cups coconut in medium bowl; set aside.

2 Combine cake mix, egg, oil, water and almond extract in large bowl. Beat at low speed with electric mixer. Stir in remaining 1⅓ cups reserved coconut. Drop rounded teaspoonful dough into reserved coconut. Roll to cover lightly. Place on ungreased baking sheet. Repeat with remaining dough, placing balls 2 inches apart. Bake at 350°F 10 to 12 minutes or until light golden brown. Cool 1 minute on baking sheets. Remove to cooling racks. Cool completely. Store in airtight container. *3½ dozen cookies*

Tip: To save time when forming dough into balls, use a 1-inch spring-operated cookie scoop. Spring-operated cookie scoops are available at kitchen specialty shops.

CHEWY FUDGE BROWNIES

1 package Duncan Hines® Chewy Fudge Brownie Mix (19.8 ounces)
1 egg
1 tablespoon water
⅓ cup MOTT'S® Natural Apple Sauce

1 Preheat oven to 350°F. Lightly grease 13×9-inch pan.

2 Follow instructions on box for PREPARE and MAKE BATTER. Spread batter in pan. Bake at 350°F 23 to 26 minutes or until set. Cool completely. *20 brownies*

Tip: If using a 9×9-inch pan, bake brownies 33 to 36 minutes; if using an 8×8-inch pan, bake brownies 34 to 37 minutes.

COCONUT CLOUDS

BEAT THE CLOCK CAKES

STRAWBERRY VANILLA CAKE

1 package Duncan Hines® Moist Deluxe® French Vanilla Cake Mix
1 container Duncan Hines® Creamy Homestyle Vanilla Buttercream Frosting, divided
⅓ cup seedless strawberry jam
Fresh strawberries, for garnish (optional)

1 Preheat oven to 350°F. Grease and flour two 8- or 9-inch round pans.

2 Prepare, bake and cool cakes following package directions for basic recipe.

3 To assemble, place one cake layer on serving plate. Place ¼ cup Vanilla frosting in small resealable plastic bag. Snip off one corner. Pipe a bead of frosting on top of layer around outer edge. Fill remaining area with strawberry jam. Top with second cake layer. Spread remaining frosting on sides and top of cake. Decorate with fresh strawberries, if desired.

12 to 16 servings

Tip: You may substitute Duncan Hines® Vanilla or Cream Cheese frosting for the Vanilla Buttercream frosting, if desired.

CHOCOLATE SPRINKLE ANGEL FOOD CAKE

1 package Duncan Hines® Angel Food Cake Mix
3 tablespoons chocolate sprinkles

1 Remove top rack from oven; move remaining rack to lowest position. Preheat oven to 350°F.

2 Prepare batter following package directions. Fold in chocolate sprinkles. Pour batter into ungreased 10-inch tube pan. Bake and cool following package directions.

12 to 16 servings

Tip: For a quick finish, simply dust cake with confectioners sugar.

TAKE-ALONG CAKE

1 package Duncan Hines® Moist Deluxe® Swiss Chocolate Cake Mix
1 package (12 ounces) semi-sweet chocolate chips
1 cup miniature marshmallows
¼ cup butter or margarine, melted
½ cup firmly packed brown sugar
½ cup chopped pecans or walnuts

1 Preheat oven to 350°F. Grease and flour 13×9×2-inch pan.

2 Prepare cake following package directions for basic recipe. Add chocolate chips and marshmallows to batter. Pour into pan. Drizzle melted butter over batter. Sprinkle with brown sugar and top with nuts. Bake at 350°F 45 to 55 minutes. Serve warm or cool completely. *12 to 16 servings*

Tip: Chocolate should be stored in a cool, dry place. When the storage area becomes too warm, chocolate will develop "bloom," a visible gray coating. Bloom has no effect on either the flavor or the quality of the chocolate and you may still use the chocolate in baking with excellent results.

CHOCOLATE SPRINKLE ANGEL FOOD CAKE

SIMPLE BOSTON CREAM PIES

1 package Duncan Hines® Moist Deluxe® Yellow Cake Mix
4 containers (3½ ounces each) ready-to-eat vanilla pudding
1 container Duncan Hines® Creamy Homestyle Chocolate Frosting

1 Preheat oven to 350°F. Grease and flour two 8- or 9-inch round pans.

2 Prepare, bake and cool cake following package directions for basic recipe.

3 To assemble, place each cake layer on serving plate. Split layers in half horizontally. Spread contents of 2 containers of vanilla pudding on bottom layer of one cake. Place top layer on filling. Repeat for second cake layer. Remove lid and foil top of Chocolate frosting container. Heat in microwave oven at HIGH (100% power) 25 to 30 seconds. Stir. (Mixture should be thin.) Spread half the chocolate glaze over top of each cake. Refrigerate until ready to serve.

12 to 16 servings

Tip: For a richer flavor, substitute Duncan Hines® Butter Recipe Golden cake mix in place of Yellow cake mix.

CHOCOLATE MARBLE ANGEL FOOD CAKE

1 package Duncan Hines® Angel Food Cake Mix
3 tablespoons chocolate syrup

1 Remove top rack from oven; move remaining rack to lowest position. Preheat oven to 350°F.

2 Prepare batter following package directions for basic recipe. Remove half the batter to another bowl; set aside. Add chocolate syrup to batter. Fold gently until blended. Alternate large spoonfuls of white and chocolate batters in ungreased 10-inch tube pan. Bake and cool following package directions.

12 to 16 servings

Tip: Serve slices drizzled with chocolate syrup for extra chocolate flavor.

SIMPLE BOSTON CREAM PIE

DOUBLE FUDGE MARBLE CAKE

1 package Duncan Hines® Moist Deluxe® Fudge Marble Cake Mix
1 container Duncan Hines® Creamy Homestyle Milk Chocolate Frosting
¼ cup hot fudge topping

1 Preheat oven to 350°F. Grease and flour 13×9×2-inch pan.

2 Prepare, bake and cool cake following package directions for basic recipe.

3 Frost top of cooled cake with Milk Chocolate frosting. Place hot fudge topping in small microwave-safe bowl. Microwave at HIGH (100% power) 30 seconds or until thin. Drop hot fudge by spoonfuls on top of cake in 18 places. Pull tip of knife once through each hot fudge dollop to form heart shapes.

12 to 16 servings

Tip: Hot fudge topping may also be marbled in frosting by using flat blade of knife to swirl slightly.

CREAMY SWISS POUND CAKE

CAKE

1 package Duncan Hines® Moist Deluxe® Swiss Chocolate Cake Mix
1 package (4-serving size) chocolate instant pudding and pie filling mix
4 eggs
1¼ cups milk
½ cup Crisco® Vegetable Oil
1 cup mini semi-sweet chocolate chips

TOPPING

1 cup whipping cream
¼ cup granulated sugar
½ teaspoon vanilla extract
Fresh raspberries, for garnish (optional)
Mini semi-sweet chocolate chips, for garnish (optional)

1 Preheat oven to 350°F. Grease and flour 10-inch Bundt® or tube pan.

2 **For cake,** combine cake mix, pudding mix, eggs, milk and oil in large bowl. Beat at low speed with electric mixer until moistened. Beat at medium speed 2 minutes. Stir in 1 cup chocolate chips. Pour into pan. Bake at 350°F 50 to 60 minutes or until toothpick inserted in center comes out clean. Cool in pan 25 minutes. Invert onto cooling rack. Cool completely.

3 **For topping,** place whipping cream, sugar and vanilla in medium bowl. Beat at high speed with electric mixer until stiff peaks form. Spoon whipped cream mixture on top of cooled cake. Garnish with fresh raspberries and chocolate chips, if desired. Refrigerate leftovers. *12 to 16 servings*

COUNTRY OVEN CARROT CAKE

1 package Duncan Hines® Moist Deluxe® Yellow Cake Mix
4 eggs
3 cups grated carrots
1 cup finely chopped nuts
½ cup Crisco® Vegetable Oil
2 teaspoons ground cinnamon
1 container Duncan Hines® Creamy Homestyle Cream Cheese Frosting

1 Preheat oven to 350°F. Grease and flour 13×9×2-inch pan (see Tip).

2 Combine cake mix, eggs, carrots, nuts, oil and cinnamon in large bowl. Beat at low speed with electric mixer until moistened. Beat at medium speed 2 minutes. Pour into pan. Bake at 350°F 40 to 45 minutes or until toothpick inserted in center comes out clean. Cool completely. Frost cake with Cream Cheese frosting. *12 to 16 servings*

Tip: Carrot cake can also be baked in two 8- or 9-inch round cake pans at 350°F 35 to 40 minutes or until toothpick inserted in center comes out clean. Cool cakes following package directions. Fill and frost cooled cakes. Garnish with whole pecans.

CHOCOLATE BANANA CAKE

CAKE

- 1 package Duncan Hines® Moist Deluxe® Devil's Food Cake Mix
- 3 eggs
- 1⅓ cups milk
- ½ cup Crisco® Vegetable Oil

TOPPING

- 1 package (4-serving size) banana cream instant pudding and pie filling mix
- 1 cup milk
- 1 cup whipping cream, whipped
- 1 medium banana
- Lemon juice
- Chocolate sprinkles

1 Preheat oven to 350°F. Grease and flour 13×9×2-inch pan.

2 **For cake,** combine cake mix, eggs, milk and oil in large bowl. Beat at low speed with electric mixer until moistened. Beat at medium speed 2 minutes. Pour into pan. Bake at 350°F 35 to 38 minutes or until toothpick inserted in center comes out clean. Cool completely.

3 **For topping,** combine pudding mix and milk in large bowl. Stir until smooth. Fold in whipped cream. Spread on top of cooled cake. Slice banana; dip in lemon juice, arrange on top. Garnish with chocolate sprinkles. Refrigerate until ready to serve. *12 to 16 servings*

Tip: A wire whisk is a great utensil to use when making instant pudding. It quickly eliminates all lumps.

STRAWBERRY STRIPE REFRIGERATOR CAKE

CAKE

- **1 package Duncan Hines® Moist Deluxe® White Cake Mix**
- **2 packages (10 ounces) frozen sweetened strawberry slices, thawed**

TOPPING

- **1 package (4-serving) vanilla instant pudding and pie filling mix**
- **1 cup milk**
- **1 cup whipping cream, whipped**
- **Fresh strawberries, for garnish (optional)**

1 Preheat oven to 350°F. Grease and flour 13×9×2-inch pan.

2 **For cake,** prepare, bake and cool following package directions. Poke holes 1 inch apart in top of cake using handle of wooden spoon. Puree thawed strawberries with juice in blender or food processor. Spoon evenly over top of cake, allowing mixture to soak into holes.

3 **For topping,** combine pudding mix and milk in large bowl. Stir until smooth. Fold in whipped cream. Spread over cake. Decorate with fresh strawberries, if desired. Refrigerate at least 4 hours. *12 to 16 servings*

Tip: For a Neapolitan Refrigerator Cake, replace the White Cake Mix with Duncan Hines® Moist Deluxe® Devil's Food Cake Mix and follow directions listed above.

YELLOW CAKE

1 package Duncan Hines® Moist Deluxe® Yellow Cake Mix*
3 eggs
1 cup water
⅓ cup MOTT'S® Natural Apple Sauce

**Follow these instructions for these flavors of Duncan Hines® Moist Deluxe® Cake Mix: Lemon Supreme, Fudge Marble, Pineapple Supreme, Spice, Strawberry Supreme, French Vanilla, Banana Supreme and Orange Supreme.*

1 Preheat oven to 350°F. Lightly grease 13×9×2-inch pan.

2 Follow instructions on box for PREPARE and MIX BATTER. Pour into pan. Bake at 350°F 31 to 34 minutes or until toothpick inserted in center comes out clean. Cool completely.

12 to 16 servings

- Two 8-inch rounds—32 to 35 minutes
- Two 9-inch rounds—27 to 30 minutes
- One 10-inch Bundt®—36 to 41 minutes
- 24 cupcakes—17 to 20 minutes

DEVIL'S FOOD CAKE

1 package Duncan Hines® Moist Deluxe® Devil's Food Cake Mix*
3 eggs
1 cup water
½ cup MOTT'S® Natural Apple Sauce

**Follow these instructions for these flavors of Duncan Hines® Moist Deluxe® Cake Mix: Swiss Chocolate, Dark Chocolate Fudge and Chocolate Mocha.*

1 Preheat oven to 350°F. Lightly grease 13×9×2-inch pan.

2 Follow instructions on box for PREPARE and MIX BATTER. Pour into pan. Bake at 350°F 34 to 37 minutes or until toothpick inserted in center comes out clean. Cool completely.

12 to 16 servings

- Two 8-inch rounds—34 to 37 minutes
- Two 9-inch rounds—29 to 32 minutes
- One 10-inch Bundt®—43 to 48 minutes
- 24 cupcakes—19 to 22 minutes

QUICK ROCKY ROAD CAKE

1 package Duncan Hines® Moist Deluxe® Devil's Food Cake Mix
1 container Duncan Hines® Creamy Homestyle Vanilla Frosting
½ cup Jif® Creamy Peanut Butter
⅓ cup semi-sweet chocolate chips
⅓ cup salted cocktail peanuts

1 Preheat oven to 350°F. Grease and flour 13×9×2-inch pan.

2 Prepare, bake and cool cake following package directions for basic recipe.

3 Combine Vanilla frosting and peanut butter in medium bowl. Frost top of cake. Sprinkle with chocolate chips and peanuts. *12 to 16 servings*

Tip: For an easy treat for kids, follow package directions for making cupcakes. Frost and decorate as directed above.

ORANGE SOAK CAKE

CAKE
1 package Duncan Hines® Moist Deluxe® Orange Supreme Cake Mix

GLAZE
2 cups confectioners sugar
⅓ cup orange juice
2 tablespoons melted butter or margarine
1 tablespoon water

1 Preheat oven to 350°F. Grease and flour 13×9×2-inch pan.

2 **For cake,** prepare and bake following package directions for basic recipe. Poke holes in top of warm cake with tines of fork or toothpick.

3 **For glaze,** combine confectioners sugar, orange juice, melted butter and water in medium bowl. Pour slowly over top allowing glaze to soak into warm cake. Cool completely. *12 to 16 servings*

Tip: Sift confectioners sugar before preparing glaze.

CHOCOLATE PEANUT BUTTER CUPS

1 package Duncan Hines® Moist Deluxe® Swiss Chocolate Cake Mix
1 container Duncan Hines® Creamy Homestyle Vanilla Frosting
½ cup Jif® Creamy Peanut Butter
15 miniature peanut butter cup candies, wrappers removed, cut in half vertically

1 Preheat oven to 350°F. Place 30 (2½-inch) paper liners in muffin cups.

2 Prepare, bake and cool cupcakes following package directions for basic recipe.

3 Combine Vanilla frosting and peanut butter in medium bowl. Stir until smooth. Frost one cupcake. Decorate with peanut butter cup candy, cut-side down. Repeat with remaining cupcakes.

30 servings

Tip: You may substitute Duncan Hines® Moist Deluxe® Devil's Food, Dark Chocolate Fudge or Butter Recipe Fudge Cake Mix flavors for Swiss Chocolate Cake Mix.

REFRESHING LEMON CAKE

1 package Duncan Hines® Moist Deluxe® Butter Recipe Golden Cake Mix
1 container Duncan Hines® Creamy Homestyle Cream Cheese Frosting
¾ cup purchased lemon curd
Lemon drop candies, crushed, for garnish (optional)

1. Preheat oven to 375°F. Grease and flour two 8- or 9-inch round cake pans.

2. Prepare, bake and cool cake following package directions for basic recipe.

3. To assemble, place one cake layer on serving plate. Place ¼ cup Cream Cheese frosting in small resealable plastic bag. Snip off one corner. Pipe a bead of frosting on top of layer around outer edge. Fill remaining area with lemon curd. Top with second cake layer. Spread remaining frosting on sides and top of cake. Garnish top of cake with crushed lemon candies, if desired.

12 to 16 servings

Tip: You may substitute Duncan Hines® Vanilla or Vanilla Buttercream frosting for the Cream Cheese frosting, if desired.

EASIEST-EVER MUFFINS & QUICK BREADS

BERRY FILLED MUFFINS

1 package Duncan Hines® Blueberry Muffin Mix
1 egg
½ cup water
¼ cup strawberry jam
2 tablespoons sliced almonds

1 Preheat oven to 400°F. Place 2½-inch paper or foil liners in 8 muffin cups.

2 Rinse blueberries from Mix with cold water and drain.

3 Empty muffin mix into bowl. Break up any lumps. Add egg and water. Stir until moistened, about 50 strokes. Fill cups half full with batter.

4 Fold blueberries into strawberry jam. Spoon on top of batter in each cup. Spread gently. Cover with remaining batter. Sprinkle with almonds. Bake at 400°F 17 to 20 minutes or until set and golden brown. Cool in pan 5 to 10 minutes. Carefully loosen muffins from pan. Remove to cooling racks. Serve warm or cool completely. *8 muffins*

Tip: For a delicious flavor variation, try using blackberry or red raspberry jam.

BERRY FILLED MUFFINS

ORANGE CINNAMON SWIRL BREAD

BREAD

- **1 package Duncan Hines® Cinnamon Swirl Muffin Mix**
- **1 egg**
- **⅔ cup orange juice**
- **1 tablespoon grated orange peel**

ORANGE GLAZE

- **½ cup confectioners sugar**
- **2 to 3 teaspoons orange juice**
- **1 teaspoon grated orange peel**
- **Quartered orange slices, for garnish (optional)**

1 Preheat oven to 350°F. Grease and flour 8½×4½×2½-inch loaf pan.

2 **For bread,** combine muffin mix and contents of topping packet from Mix in large bowl. Break up any lumps. Add egg, ⅔ cup orange juice and 1 tablespoon orange peel. Stir until moistened, about 50 strokes. Knead swirl packet from Mix for 10 seconds before opening. Squeeze contents on top of batter. Swirl into batter with knife or spatula, folding from bottom of bowl to get an even swirl. DO NOT COMPLETELY MIX IN. Pour into pan. Bake at 350°F 55 to 60 minutes or until toothpick inserted in center comes out clean. Cool in pan 10 minutes. Loosen loaf from pan. Invert onto cooling rack. Turn right side up. Cool completely.

3 **For orange glaze,** place confectioners sugar in small bowl. Add orange juice, 1 teaspoon at a time, stirring until smooth and desired consistency. Stir in 1 teaspoon orange peel. Drizzle over loaf. Garnish with orange slices, if desired.

1 loaf (12 slices)

Tip: If glaze becomes too thin, add more confectioners sugar. If glaze is too thick, add more orange juice.

LEMON BLUEBERRY LOAF

BREAD

- **1 package Duncan Hines® Blueberry Muffin Mix**
- **1 egg**
- **½ cup dairy sour cream**
- **½ cup milk**
- **1 tablespoon grated lemon peel**
- **½ cup chopped pecans**

GLAZE

- **⅓ cup granulated sugar**
- **2 tablespoons lemon juice**

1 Preheat oven to 350°F. Grease and flour 9×5-inch loaf pan.

2 Rinse blueberries from Mix with cold water and drain.

3 **For bread,** empty muffin mix into medium bowl. Break up any lumps. Add egg, sour cream, milk and grated lemon peel. Stir until moistened, about 50 strokes. Fold in blueberries and pecans. Pour into pan. Bake at 350°F 60 to 65 minutes or until toothpick inserted in center comes out clean. Poke holes in top of warm loaf with toothpick or long-tined fork.

4 **For glaze,** combine sugar and lemon juice in small saucepan. Cook on medium heat, stirring constantly, until sugar dissolves. Spoon hot glaze evenly over loaf. Cool in pan 15 minutes. Loosen loaf from pan. Invert onto cooling rack. Turn right side up. Cool completely. *1 loaf (12 slices)*

Tip: When grating lemon peel, avoid the bitter white portion known as the pith.

CARAMEL PECAN SPICE CAKES

- **1 package Duncan Hines® Moist Deluxe® Spice Cake Mix**
- **1 package (4-serving size) vanilla instant pudding and pie filling mix**
- **4 eggs**
- **1 cup water**
- **⅓ cup Crisco® Vegetable Oil**
- **1½ cups pecan pieces, toasted and finely chopped (see Tip)**
- **1 container Duncan Hines® Creamy Homestyle Caramel Frosting**

1 Preheat oven to 350°F. Grease and flour two 8½×4½×2½-inch loaf pans.

2 Combine cake mix, pudding mix, eggs, water and oil in large bowl. Beat at low speed with electric mixer until moistened. Beat at medium speed 2 minutes. Stir in toasted pecans. Pour batter into pans. Bake at 350°F 55 to 60 minutes or until toothpick inserted in center comes out clean. Cool in pans 15 minutes. Loosen loaves from pans. Invert onto cooling rack. Turn right sides up. Cool completely.

3 Spread Caramel frosting evenly on cooled loaves. Garnish with pecan halves and maraschino cherry halves before glaze sets. *2 loaves (24 slices)*

Tip: To toast pecans, spread pecan pieces evenly on baking sheet. Toast in 350°F oven about 8 minutes or until fragrant. Cool completely.

BLUEBERRY ORANGE MUFFINS

1 package Duncan Hines® Blueberry Muffin Mix
2 egg whites
½ cup orange juice
1 teaspoon grated orange peel

1 Preheat oven to 400°F. Grease 2½-inch muffin cups (or use paper liners).

2 Rinse blueberries from Mix with cold water and drain.

3 Empty muffin mix into large bowl. Break up any lumps. Add egg whites, orange juice and orange peel. Stir until moistened, about 50 strokes. Fold blueberries gently into batter.

4 For large muffins, fill cups two-thirds full. Bake at 400°F 18 to 21 minutes or until toothpick inserted in center comes out clean. (For medium muffins, fill cups half full. Bake at 400°F 16 to 19 minutes or until toothpick inserted in center comes out clean.) Cool in pan 5 to 10 minutes. Carefully loosen muffins from pan. Remove to cooling racks. Serve warm or cool completely. *8 large or 12 medium muffins*

Tip: Freeze extra grated orange peel for future use.

CRANBERRY PECAN MUFFINS

1½ cups fresh or frozen cranberries
¼ cup light corn syrup
1 package Duncan Hines® Cinnamon Swirl Muffin Mix
1 egg
¾ cup water or milk
½ cup chopped pecans

1 Preheat oven to 400°F. Place 14 (2½-inch) paper liners in muffin cups (see Tip). Place cranberries and corn syrup in heavy saucepan. Cook on medium heat, stirring occasionally, until cranberries pop and mixture is slightly thickened. Drain cranberries in small strainer; set aside.

2 Empty muffin mix into medium bowl. Break up any lumps. Add egg and water. Stir until moistened, about 50 strokes. Stir in cranberries and pecans. Knead swirl packet from Mix for 10 seconds before opening. Cut off 1 end of swirl packet. Squeeze contents over top of batter. Swirl into batter with knife or spatula. DO NOT COMPLETELY MIX IN. Spoon batter into muffin cups (see Tip). Sprinkle with contents of topping packet from Mix. Bake at 400°F 18 to 22 minutes or until toothpick inserted in center comes out clean. Cool in pans 5 to 10 minutes. Remove to cooling racks. Serve warm or cool completely.

14 muffins

Tip: Fill an equal number of muffin cups in each muffin pan with batter. For more even baking, fill empty muffin cups with ½ inch of water.

SOCK-IT-TO-ME CAKE

STREUSEL FILLING

- 1 package Duncan Hines® Moist Deluxe® Butter Recipe Golden Cake Mix, divided
- 2 tablespoons brown sugar
- 2 teaspoons ground cinnamon
- 1 cup finely chopped pecans

CAKE

- 4 eggs
- 1 cup dairy sour cream
- ⅓ cup Crisco® Vegetable Oil
- ¼ cup water
- ¼ cup granulated sugar

GLAZE

- 1 cup confectioners sugar
- 1 or 2 tablespoons milk

1 Preheat oven to 375°F. Grease and flour 10-inch tube pan.

2 **For streusel filling,** combine 2 tablespoons cake mix, brown sugar and cinnamon in medium bowl. Stir in pecans. Set aside.

3 **For cake,** combine remaining cake mix, eggs, sour cream, oil, water and granulated sugar in large bowl. Beat at medium speed with electric mixer 2 minutes. Pour two-thirds of batter into pan. Sprinkle with streusel filling. Spoon remaining batter evenly over filling. Bake at 375°F 45 to 55 minutes or until toothpick inserted in center comes out clean. Cool in pan 25 minutes. Invert onto serving plate. Cool completely.

4 **For glaze,** combine confectioners sugar and milk in small bowl. Stir until smooth. Drizzle over cake.

12 to 16 servings

Tip: For a quick glaze, place ½ cup Duncan Hines® Creamy Homestyle Vanilla Frosting in small microwave-safe bowl. Microwave at HIGH (100% power) 10 seconds; add 5 to 10 seconds, if needed. Stir until smooth and thin.

SPRING BREAK BLUEBERRY COFFEECAKE

TOPPING

- **½ cup flaked coconut**
- **¼ cup firmly packed brown sugar**
- **2 tablespoons butter or margarine, softened**
- **1 tablespoon all-purpose flour**

CAKE

- **1 package Duncan Hines® Blueberry Muffin Mix**
- **1 can (8 ounces) crushed pineapple with juice, undrained**
- **1 egg**
- **¼ cup water**

1. Preheat oven to 350°F. Grease 9-inch square pan.

2. **For topping,** combine coconut, brown sugar, butter and flour in small bowl. Mix with fork until well blended. Set aside.

3. Rinse blueberries from Mix with cold water and drain.

4. **For cake,** empty muffin mix into medium bowl. Break up any lumps. Add pineapple with juice, egg and water. Stir until moistened, about 50 strokes. Fold in blueberries. Spread in pan. Sprinkle reserved topping over batter. Bake at 350°F 30 to 35 minutes or until toothpick inserted in center comes out clean. Serve warm or cool completely. *9 servings*

Tip: To keep blueberries from discoloring batter, drain on paper towels after rinsing.

COCONUT CHOCOLATE CHIP LOAF

- 1 package Duncan Hines® Chocolate Chip Muffin Mix
- 1⅓ cups toasted flaked coconut (see Tip)
- 1 egg
- ¾ cup water
- ½ teaspoon vanilla extract
- Confectioners sugar, for garnish (optional)

1 Preheat oven to 350°F. Grease and flour 9×5×3-inch loaf pan.

2 Empty muffin mix into medium bowl. Break up any lumps. Add coconut, egg, water and vanilla extract. Stir until moistened, about 50 strokes. Pour into pan. Bake at 350°F 45 to 50 minutes or until toothpick inserted in center comes out clean. Cool in pan 15 minutes. Invert onto cooling rack. Turn right side up. Cool completely. Dust with confectioners sugar, if desired.

1 loaf (12 slices)

Tip: Spread coconut evenly on baking sheet. Toast at 350°F 5 minutes. Stir and toast 1 to 2 minutes longer or until light golden brown.

Duncan Hines®

KIDS CAN-DO!

BANANA SPLIT CAKE

- 1 package Duncan Hines® Moist Deluxe® Banana Supreme Cake Mix
- 3 eggs
- 1⅓ cups water
- ½ cup all-purpose flour
- ⅓ cup Crisco® Vegetable Oil
- 1 cup semi-sweet mini chocolate chips
- 2 to 3 bananas
- 1 can (16 ounces) chocolate syrup
- 1 container (8 ounces) frozen whipped topping, thawed
- ½ cup chopped walnuts
- Colored sprinkles
- Maraschino cherries with stems, for garnish

1 Preheat oven to 350°F. Grease and flour 13×9×2-inch pan.

2 Combine cake mix, eggs, water, flour and oil in large bowl. Beat at low speed with electric mixer until moistened. Beat at medium speed 2 minutes. Stir in chocolate chips. Pour into pan. Bake at 350°F 32 to 35 minutes or until toothpick inserted in center comes out clean. Cool completely.

3 Slice bananas. Cut cake into squares; top with banana slices. Drizzle with chocolate syrup. Top with whipped topping, walnuts and sprinkles. Garnish with maraschino cherries. *12 to 16 servings*

Tip: Dip bananas in diluted lemon juice to prevent darkening.

ICE CREAM CONE CAKES

1 package Duncan Hines® Moist Deluxe® Cake Mix (any flavor)
1 container Duncan Hines® Creamy Homestyle Chocolate Frosting
1 container Duncan Hines® Creamy Homestyle Vanilla Frosting
Chocolate sprinkles
Assorted decors
Jelly beans
2 maraschino cherries, for garnish

1 Preheat oven to 350°F. Grease and flour one 8-inch round cake pan and one 8-inch square pan.

2 Prepare cake following package directions for basic recipe. Pour about 2 cups batter into round pan. Pour about 3 cups batter into square pan. Bake at 350°F 30 to 35 minutes or until toothpick inserted in center comes out clean. Cool following package directions.

3 To assemble, cut cooled cake and arrange as shown. Frost "cone" with Chocolate frosting, reserving ½ cup. Place writing tip in pastry bag. Fill with remaining ½ cup Chocolate frosting. Pipe waffle pattern onto "cones." Decorate with chocolate sprinkles. Spread Vanilla frosting on "ice cream" parts. Decorate with assorted decors and jelly beans. Top each with maraschino cherry. *12 to 16 servings*

Tip: Use tip of knife to draw lines in frosting for waffle pattern as guide for piping chocolate frosting.

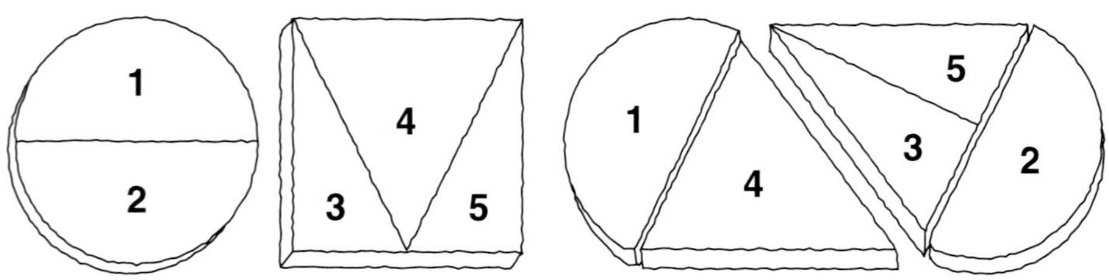

PORCUPINE CUPCAKES

1 package Duncan Hines® Moist Deluxe® Cake Mix (any flavor)
1 container Duncan Hines® Creamy Homestyle Chocolate Frosting
Sliced almonds

1 Preheat oven to 350°F. Place 2½-inch paper liners in 24 muffin cups.

2 Prepare, bake and cool cupcakes following package directions for basic recipe. Frost cupcakes with Chocolate frosting. Place sliced almonds upright on each cupcake to decorate as a "porcupine." *24 cupcakes*

Tip: Slivered almonds can be used in place of sliced almonds.

BROWNIE CANDY CUPS

1 package Duncan Hines® Double Fudge Brownie Mix
2 eggs
⅓ cup water
¼ cup Crisco® Vegetable Oil
30 miniature peanut butter cup candies, wrappers removed

1 Preheat oven to 350°F. Place 30 (2-inch) foil liners in muffin pans or on baking sheets.

2 Combine brownie mix, fudge packet from Mix, eggs, water and oil in large bowl. Stir with spoon until well blended, about 50 strokes. Place 2 level measuring tablespoons batter in each foil liner. Bake at 350°F 10 minutes. Remove from oven. Push 1 peanut butter cup candy in center of each cupcake until even with surface of brownie. Bake 5 to 7 minutes longer. Remove to cooling racks. Cool completely. *30 brownie cups*

Tip: Pack these brownies in your child's lunch bag for a special treat.

CAPTIVATING CATERPILLAR CUPCAKES

1 package Duncan Hines® Moist Deluxe® White Cake Mix
3 egg whites
1⅓ cups water
2 tablespoons Crisco® Vegetable Oil
½ cup star decors, divided
1 container Duncan Hines® Creamy Homestyle Vanilla Frosting
Green food coloring
6 chocolate sandwich cookies, finely crushed (see Tip)
½ cup candy-coated chocolate pieces
⅓ cup assorted jelly beans
Assorted nonpareil decors

1 Preheat oven to 350°F. Place 24 (2½-inch) paper liners in muffin cups.

2 Combine cake mix, egg whites, water and oil in large bowl. Beat at low speed with electric mixer until moistened. Beat at medium speed 2 minutes. Fold in ⅓ cup star decors. Fill paper liners about half full. Bake at 350°F 18 to 23 minutes or until toothpick inserted in center comes out clean. Cool in pans 5 minutes. Remove to cooling racks. Cool completely.

3 Tint Vanilla frosting with green food coloring. Frost one cupcake. Sprinkle ½ teaspoon chocolate cookie crumbs on frosting. Arrange 4 candy-coated chocolate pieces to form caterpillar body. Place jelly bean at one end to form head. Attach remaining star and nonpareil decors with dots of frosting to form eyes. Repeat with remaining cupcakes.

24 cupcakes

Tip: To finely crush chocolate sandwich cookies, place cookies in resealable plastic bag. Remove excess air from bag; seal. Press rolling pin on top of cookies to break into pieces. Continue pressing until evenly crushed.

BACK-TO-SCHOOL PENCIL CAKE

1 package Duncan Hines® Moist Deluxe® Cake Mix (any flavor)
2 containers Duncan Hines® Creamy Homestyle Vanilla Frosting, divided
Red and yellow food coloring
Chocolate sprinkles

1 Preheat oven to 350°F. Grease and flour 13×9×2-inch pan.

2 Prepare, bake and cool cake following package directions for basic recipe.

3 For frosting, tint 1 cup Vanilla frosting pink with red food coloring. Tint remaining frosting with yellow food coloring.

4 To assemble, cut cooled cake and arrange on large baking sheet or piece of sturdy cardboard as shown. Spread pink frosting on cake for eraser at one end and for wood at other end. Spread yellow frosting over remaining cake. Decorate with chocolate sprinkles for pencil tip and eraser band (see Photo). *12 to 16 servings*

Tip: To make this cake even more special, reserve 1/4 cup Vanilla frosting before tinting yellow. Place writing tip in decorating bag. Fill with frosting. Pipe name of child, teacher or school on pencil.

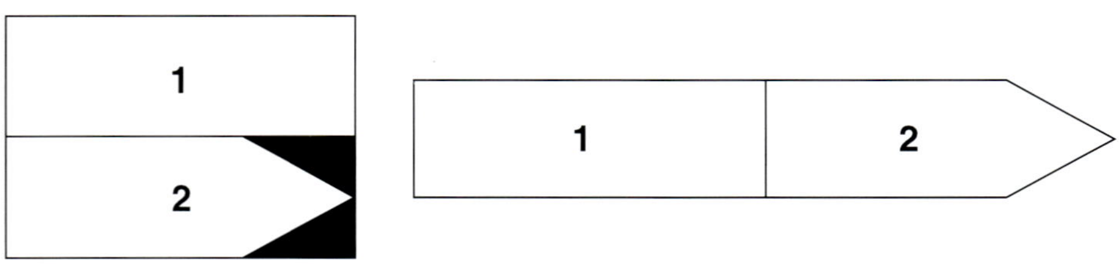

yellow-green
RUBBER STAMPS

CHOCOLATE BUNNY COOKIES

1 package Duncan Hines® Chewy Fudge Brownie Mix (19.8 ounces)
1 egg
¼ cup water
¼ cup Crisco® Vegetable Oil
1⅓ cups pecan halves (96)
1 container Duncan Hines® Creamy Homestyle Dark Chocolate Fudge Frosting
Vanilla milk chips

1 Preheat oven to 350°F. Grease baking sheets.

2 Combine brownie mix, egg, water and oil in large bowl. Stir with spoon until well blended, about 50 strokes. Drop by 2 level teaspoonfuls 2 inches apart on greased baking sheets. Place two pecan halves, flat-side up, on each cookie for ears. Bake at 350°F 10 to 12 minutes or until set. Cool 2 minutes on baking sheets. Remove to cooling racks. Cool completely.

3 Spread Dark Chocolate Fudge frosting on one cookie. Place vanilla milk chips, upside down, on frosting for eyes and nose. Dot each eye with frosting using toothpick. Repeat for remaining cookies. Allow frosting to set before storing cookies between layers of waxed paper in airtight container.

4 dozen cookies

Tip: For variety, frost cookies with Duncan Hines® Vanilla Frosting and use semi-sweet chocolate chips for the eyes and noses.

FOOTBALL CAKE

1 package Duncan Hines® Moist Deluxe® Devil's Food Cake Mix

DECORATOR FROSTING

¾ cup confectioners sugar
2 tablespoons Crisco® Shortening
1 tablespoon cold water
1 tablespoon non-dairy powdered creamer
¼ teaspoon vanilla extract
Dash salt
1 container Duncan Hines® Creamy Homestyle Chocolate Frosting

1 Preheat oven to 350°F. Grease and flour 10-inch round cake pan. Prepare cake following package directions for basic recipe. Bake at 350°F 45 to 55 minutes or until toothpick inserted in center comes out clean.

2 **For decorator frosting,** combine confectioners sugar, shortening, water, non-dairy powdered creamer, vanilla extract and salt in small bowl. Beat at medium speed with electric mixer 2 minutes. Add more confectioners sugar to thicken or water to thin frosting as needed.

3 Cut cake and remove 2-inch slice from center. Arrange cake as shown. Spread chocolate frosting on sides and top of cake. Place basketweave tip in pastry bag. Fill with decorator frosting. Make white frosting laces on football.

12 to 16 servings

Tip: If a 10-inch round pan is not available, make 2 football cakes by following package directions for baking with two 9-inch round cake pans.

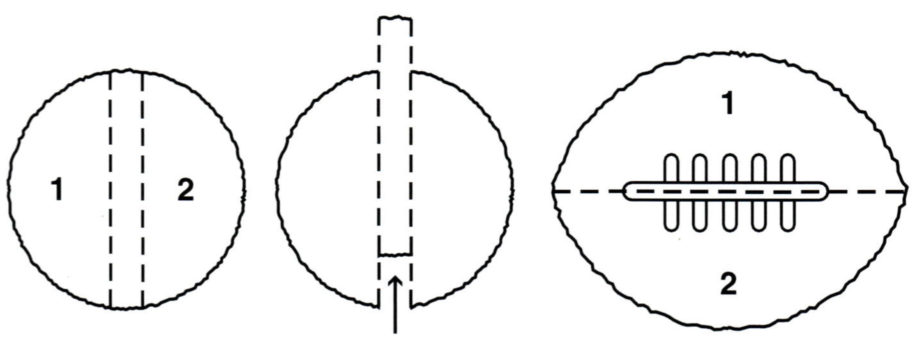

BERRY SURPRISE CUPCAKES

1 package Duncan Hines® Moist Deluxe® White Cake Mix
3 egg whites
1⅓ cups water
2 tablespoons Crisco® Vegetable Oil
3 sheets (0.5 ounce each) strawberry chewy fruit snacks
1 container Duncan Hines® Creamy Homestyle Vanilla Frosting
2 pouches (0.9 ounce each) chewy fruit snack shapes, for garnish (optional)

1 Preheat oven to 350°F. Place 24 (2½-inch) paper liners in muffin cups.

2 Combine cake mix, egg whites, water and oil in large bowl. Beat at low speed with electric mixer until moistened. Beat at medium speed 2 minutes. Fill each liner half full with batter.

3 Cut three fruit snack sheets into 9 equal pieces. (You will have 3 extra squares.) Place each fruit snack piece on top of batter in each cup. Pour remaining batter equally over each. Bake at 350°F 18 to 23 minutes or until toothpick inserted in center comes out clean. Cool in pans 5 minutes. Remove to cooling racks. Cool completely. Frost cupcakes with Vanilla frosting. Decorate with fruit snack shapes, if desired.

12 to 16 servings

Tip: To make a Berry Surprise Cake, prepare cake following package directions. Pour half the batter into prepared 13×9×2-inch pan. Place 4 fruit snack sheets evenly on top. Pour remaining batter over all. Bake and cool as directed on package. Frost and decorate as described above.

Duncan Hines®

SIMPLE BUT SINFUL DESSERTS

DOUBLE BERRY LAYER CAKE

- **1 package Duncan Hines® Moist Deluxe® Strawberry Supreme Cake Mix**
- **⅔ cup strawberry jam, divided**
- **2½ cups fresh blueberries, rinsed, drained and divided**
- **1 container (8 ounces) frozen whipped topping, thawed and divided**
- **Fresh strawberry slices, for garnish**

1. Preheat oven to 350°F. Grease and flour two 9-inch round cake pans.

2. Prepare, bake and cool cake following package directions for basic recipe.

3. Place one cake layer on serving plate. Spread with ⅓ cup strawberry jam. Arrange 1 cup blueberries on jam. Spread half the whipped topping to within ½ inch of cake edge. Place second cake layer on top. Repeat with remaining ⅓ cup strawberry jam, 1 cup blueberries and remaining whipped topping. Garnish with strawberry slices and remaining ½ cup blueberries. Refrigerate until ready to serve. *12 servings*

Tip: For best results, cut cake with serrated knife; clean knife after each slice.

CHOCOLATE CHERRY TORTE

1 package Duncan Hines® Moist Deluxe® Devil's Food Cake Mix
1 can (21 ounces) cherry pie filling
¼ teaspoon almond extract
1 container (8 ounces) frozen whipped topping, thawed and divided
¼ cup toasted sliced almonds, for garnish (see Tip)

1 Preheat oven to 350°F. Grease and flour two 9-inch round cake pans.

2 Prepare, bake and cool cake following package directions for basic recipe. Combine cherry pie filling and almond extract in small bowl. Stir until blended.

3 To assemble, place one cake layer on serving plate. Spread with 1 cup whipped topping, then half the cherry pie filling mixture. Top with second cake layer. Spread remaining pie filling to within 1½ inches of cake edge. Decorate cake edge with remaining whipped topping. Garnish with sliced almonds.

12 to 16 servings

Tip: To toast almonds, spread in a single layer on baking sheet. Bake at 325°F 4 to 6 minutes or until fragrant and golden.

STRAWBERRY CELEBRATION CAKE

1 package Duncan Hines® Moist Deluxe® Strawberry Supreme Cake Mix
1 cup strawberry preserves, heated
1 container Duncan Hines® Creamy Homestyle Cream Cheese Frosting
Strawberry halves, for garnish
Mint leaves, for garnish

1 Preheat oven to 350°F. Grease and flour 10-inch Bundt® or tube pan.

2 Prepare, bake and cool cake following package directions for basic recipe.

3 Split cake horizontally into three even layers. Place bottom cake layer on serving plate. Spread with ½ cup warm preserves. Repeat layering. Top with remaining cake layer. Frost cake with Cream Cheese frosting. Garnish with strawberry halves and mint leaves. Refrigerate until ready to serve. *12 to 16 servings*

Tip: For a delicious variation, substitute 1 cup seedless red raspberry jam for the strawberry preserves.

BUTTER PECAN PIE

1 cup coarsely chopped pecans
¼ cup butter or margarine
1 container Duncan Hines® Creamy Homestyle Vanilla Buttercream Frosting
1 package (8 ounces) cream cheese, softened
1 cup frozen non-dairy whipped topping, thawed
1 prepared 9-inch graham cracker crumb pie crust
Pecan halves, for garnish

1 Place pecans and butter in 10-inch skillet on medium heat. Cook, stirring constantly, until butter is lightly browned. Pour into heat-proof large bowl. Add Vanilla frosting and cream cheese. Stir until thoroughly blended.

2 Fold in whipped topping. Pour into prepared crust. Garnish with pecan halves, if desired. Refrigerate for 4 hours or until firm. *8 to 10 servings*

HUMMINGBIRD CAKE

1 package Duncan Hines® Moist Deluxe® Yellow Cake Mix
1 package (4-serving size) vanilla instant pudding and pie filling mix
½ cup Crisco® Vegetable Oil
1 can (8 ounces) crushed pineapple, well drained (reserve juice)
Reserved pineapple juice plus water to equal 1 cup
4 eggs
1 teaspoon ground cinnamon
½ medium-size ripe banana, cut up
½ cup finely chopped pecans
¼ cup chopped maraschino cherries, well drained
Confectioners sugar

1 Preheat oven to 350°F. Grease and flour 10-inch Bundt® or tube pan.

2 Combine cake mix, pudding mix, oil, pineapple, 1 cup juice and water mixture, eggs and cinnamon in large bowl. Beat at low speed with electric mixer until moistened. Beat at medium speed 2 minutes. Stir in banana, pecans and cherries. Pour into pan. Bake at 350°F 50 to 60 minutes or until toothpick inserted in center comes out clean. Cool in pan 25 minutes. Invert onto serving plate. Sprinkle with confectioners sugar. *12 to 16 servings*

Tip: Also great with Cream Cheese Glaze. For glaze, heat 1 container Duncan Hines® Creamy Homestyle Cream Cheese frosting in microwave at HIGH (100% power) 30 seconds. Do not overheat. Stir until smooth.

FANTASY ANGEL FOOD CAKE

1 package Duncan Hines® Angel Food Cake Mix
Red and green food coloring
1 container Duncan Hines® Creamy Homestyle Cream Cheese Frosting

1 Preheat oven to 350°F.

2 Prepare cake following package directions. Divide batter into thirds and place in 3 different bowls. Add a few drops red food coloring to one. Add a few drops green food coloring to another. Stir each until well blended. Leave the third one plain. Spoon pink batter into ungreased 10-inch tube pan. Cover with white batter and top with green batter. Bake and cool following package directions.

3 To make Cream Cheese glaze, heat frosting in microwave at HIGH (100% power) 20 to 30 seconds. Do not overheat. Stir until smooth. Set aside ¼ cup warm glaze. Spoon remaining glaze on top and sides of cake to completely cover. Divide remaining glaze in half and place in 2 different bowls. Add a few drops red food coloring to one. Add a few drops green food coloring to the other. Stir each until well blended. Using a teaspoon, drizzle green glaze around edge of cake so it will run down sides. Repeat with pink glaze. *16 servings*

Tip: For marble cake, drop batter by spoonfuls, alternating colors frequently.

FANTASY ANGEL FOOD CAKE

PUMPKIN PIE CRUNCH

- 1 can (16 ounces) solid pack pumpkin
- 1 can (12 ounces) evaporated milk
- 3 eggs
- 1½ cups sugar
- 4 teaspoons pumpkin pie spice
- ½ teaspoon salt
- 1 package Duncan Hines® Moist Deluxe® Yellow Cake Mix
- 1 cup chopped pecans
- 1 cup butter or margarine, melted
- Whipped topping

1 Preheat oven to 350°F. Grease bottom of 13×9×2-inch pan.

2 Combine pumpkin, evaporated milk, eggs, sugar, pumpkin pie spice and salt in large bowl. Pour into pan. Sprinkle dry cake mix evenly over pumpkin mixture. Top with pecans. Drizzle with melted butter. Bake at 350°F 50 to 55 minutes or until golden. Cool completely. Serve with whipped topping. Refrigerate leftovers. *16 to 20 servings*

Tip: For a richer flavor, try using Duncan Hines® Moist Deluxe® Butter Recipe Golden Cake Mix.

RICH DOUBLE CHOCOLATE CREAM TORTE

BROWNIE

- 1 package Duncan Hines® Milk Chocolate Chunk Brownie Mix
- 3 eggs
- ⅓ cup water
- ⅓ cup Crisco® Vegetable Oil
- ½ cup finely chopped nuts

CHOCOLATE BUTTER CREAM

- 1 package (6 ounces) semi-sweet chocolate chips, melted
- ½ cup butter or margarine, softened
- 1 cup whipping cream, chilled and divided

WHIPPED CREAM

- 2 tablespoons sugar
- 1 tablespoon chocolate sprinkles

1 Preheat oven to 350°F. Grease and flour 9-inch round pan.

2 **For brownie,** combine brownie mix, eggs, water, oil and nuts in large bowl. Stir with spoon until well blended, about 50 strokes. Pour into pan. Bake at 350°F 35 to 40 minutes. Cool 30 minutes. Run knife around edge of pan. Invert onto serving platter. Cool completely.

3 **For chocolate butter cream,** stir together melted chocolate, butter and 2 tablespoons whipping cream. Spread over top of cooled brownie.

4 **For whipped cream,** beat remaining whipping cream and sugar in medium bowl with electric mixer on high speed 1 to 3 minutes or until thick. Spread over chocolate butter cream. Sprinkle with chocolate sprinkles. Refrigerate until ready to serve.

8 to 12 servings

Tip: Chilling the beaters and bowl before whipping the cream decreases whipping time and helps insure good volume.

LUSCIOUS KEY LIME CAKE

CAKE

- 1 package Duncan Hines® Moist Deluxe® Lemon Supreme Cake Mix
- 1 package (4-serving size) lemon instant pudding and pie filling mix
- 4 eggs
- 1 cup Crisco® Vegetable Oil
- ¾ cup water
- ¼ cup Key lime juice (see Tip)

GLAZE

- 2 cups confectioners sugar
- ⅓ cup Key lime juice
- 2 tablespoons water
- 2 tablespoons butter or margarine, melted
- Additional confectioners sugar
- Lime slices, for garnish
- Fresh strawberry slices, for garnish (optional)

1 Preheat oven to 350°F. Grease and flour 10-inch Bundt® or tube pan.

2 **For cake,** combine cake mix, pudding mix, eggs, oil, ¾ cup water and ¼ cup Key lime juice in large bowl. Beat at low speed with electric mixer until moistened. Beat at medium speed 2 minutes. Pour into pan. Bake at 350°F 50 to 60 minutes or until toothpick inserted in center comes out clean. Cool in pan 25 minutes. Remove cake from pan onto cooling rack. Return cake to pan. Poke holes in top of warm cake with toothpick or long-tined fork.

3 **For glaze,** combine 2 cups confectioners sugar, ⅓ cup Key lime juice, 2 tablespoons water and melted butter in medium bowl. Pour slowly over top of warm cake. Cool completely. Invert onto serving plate. Dust with additional confectioners sugar. Garnish with lime slices and strawberry slices, if desired. *12 to 16 servings*

Tip: Fresh or bottled lime juice may be substituted for the Key lime juice.

RICH PUMPKIN CHEESECAKE

CRUST

- **1 package Duncan Hines® Moist Deluxe® Spice Cake Mix**
- **½ cup butter or margarine, melted**

FILLING

- **3 packages (8 ounces each) cream cheese, softened**
- **1 can (14 ounces) sweetened condensed milk**
- **1 can (16 ounces) solid pack pumpkin**
- **4 eggs**
- **1 tablespoon pumpkin pie spice**

TOPPING

- **1 package (2½ ounces) sliced almonds**
- **2 cups whipping cream, chilled**
- **¼ cup sugar**

1 Preheat oven to 375°F.

2 **For crust,** combine cake mix and melted butter in large bowl; press into bottom of ungreased 10-inch springform pan.

3 **For filling,** combine cream cheese and sweetened condensed milk in large bowl. Beat with electric mixer at high speed 2 minutes. Add pumpkin, eggs and pumpkin pie spice. Beat at high speed 1 minute. Pour over prepared crust in pan. Bake at 375°F 65 to 70 minutes or until set. Cool completely on rack. Refrigerate 2 hours. Loosen cake from sides of pan; remove sides of pan.

4 **For topping,** preheat oven to 300°F. Toast almonds on baking sheet at 300°F 4 to 5 minutes or until fragrant and light golden brown. Cool completely. Beat whipping cream in medium bowl with electric mixer on high speed until soft peaks form. Gradually add sugar; beat until stiff peaks form. Spread over top of chilled cake. Garnish with toasted almonds. Refrigerate until ready to serve. *8 to 12 servings*

Tip: To prepare in 13×9×2-inch pan, bake at 350°F 35 minutes or until set.

TRIPLE CHOCOLATE FANTASY

CAKE

- **1 package Duncan Hines® Moist Deluxe® Devil's Food Cake Mix**
- **3 eggs**
- **1⅓ cups water**
- **½ cup Crisco® Vegetable Oil**
- **½ cup ground walnuts (see Tip)**

CHOCOLATE GLAZE

- **1 package (12 ounces) semi-sweet chocolate chips**
- **¼ cup plus 2 tablespoons butter or margarine**
- **¼ cup coarsely chopped walnuts**

WHITE CHOCOLATE GLAZE

- **3 ounces white chocolate, coarsely chopped**
- **1 tablespoon Crisco® Shortening**

1 Preheat oven to 350°F. Grease and flour 10-inch Bundt® pan.

2 **For cake,** combine cake mix, eggs, water, oil and ground walnuts in large bowl. Beat at low speed with electric mixer until moistened. Beat at medium speed 2 minutes. Pour into pan. Bake at 350°F 45 to 55 minutes or until toothpick inserted in center comes out clean. Cool in pan 25 minutes. Invert onto serving plate. Cool completely.

3 **For chocolate glaze,** combine chocolate chips and butter in small heavy saucepan. Heat on low heat until chips are melted. Stir constantly until shiny and smooth. (Glaze will be very thick.) Spread hot glaze over cooled cake. Sprinkle with coarsely chopped walnuts.

4 **For white chocolate glaze,** combine white chocolate and shortening in another small heavy saucepan. Heat on low heat until melted, stirring constantly. Drizzle hot glaze over top and sides of cake. *12 to 16 servings*

Tip: To grind walnuts, use a food processor fitted with steel blade. Process until fine.

HERSHEY'S® Best-Loved RECIPES

Contents

TOFFEE BITS CHEESECAKE

CHOCOLATE CRUMB CRUST (recipe follows)
3 packages (8 ounces each) cream cheese, softened
¾ cup sugar
3 eggs
1¾ cups (10-ounce package) SKOR English Toffee Bits or 1¾ cups HEATH Bits 'O Brickle, divided
1 teaspoon vanilla extract
Sweetened whipped cream

1. Prepare CHOCOLATE CRUMB CRUST; set aside. Heat oven to 350°F.

2. Beat cream cheese and sugar in large bowl until smooth. Add eggs, one at a time, beating well after each addition. Set aside 1 tablespoon toffee bits. Gently stir remaining toffee bits and vanilla into batter; pour into prepared crust.

3. Bake 45 to 50 minutes or until almost set. Remove from oven to wire rack. With knife, loosen cake from side of pan. Cool completely; remove side of pan. Cover; refrigerate. Just before serving, garnish with sweetened whipped cream and reserved toffee bits. Cover; refrigerate leftover cheesecake.

10 to 12 servings

CHOCOLATE CRUMB CRUST: Heat oven to 350°F. Stir together 1¼ cups (about 40 wafers) vanilla wafer crumbs, ⅓ cup powdered sugar and ⅓ cup HERSHEY'S Cocoa in medium bowl; stir in ¼ cup (½ stick) melted butter or margarine. Press mixture firmly onto bottom and ½ inch up side of 9-inch springform pan. Bake 8 minutes; cool slightly.

PREP TIME: 25 minutes **BAKE TIME:** 45 minutes
COOL TIME: 1 hour **CHILL TIME:** 4 hours

Toffee Bits Cheesecake

CHOCOLATETOWN SPECIAL CAKE

½ cup HERSHEY'S Cocoa or HERSHEY'S Dutch Processed Cocoa
½ cup boiling water
⅔ cup shortening
1¾ cups sugar
1 teaspoon vanilla extract
2 eggs
2¼ cups all-purpose flour
1½ teaspoons baking soda
½ teaspoon salt
1⅓ cups buttermilk or sour milk*
ONE-BOWL BUTTERCREAM FROSTING (page 169)

**To sour milk: Use 4 teaspoons white vinegar plus milk to equal 1⅓ cups.*

1. Heat oven to 350°F. Grease and flour two 9-inch round baking pans.

2. Stir together cocoa and water in small bowl until smooth. Beat shortening, sugar and vanilla in large bowl until light and fluffy. Add eggs; beat well. Stir together flour, baking soda and salt; add to shortening mixture alternately with buttermilk, beating until well blended. Add cocoa mixture; beat well. Pour batter into prepared pans.

3. Bake 35 to 40 minutes or until wooden pick inserted in center comes out clean. Cool 10 minutes; remove from pans to wire racks. Cool completely. Frost with ONE-BOWL BUTTERCREAM FROSTING.

8 to 10 servings

PREP TIME: 30 minutes **BAKE TIME:** 35 minutes **COOL TIME:** 2 hours

PEANUT BUTTER CHIP CHEESECAKE

⅓ cup butter or margarine, melted
1¼ cups graham cracker crumbs
⅓ cup HERSHEY'S Cocoa
⅓ cup sugar
1 cup REESE'S Peanut Butter Chips
2 packages (8 ounces each) cream cheese, softened
1 can (14 ounces) sweetened condensed milk (not evaporated milk)
4 eggs
1 teaspoon vanilla extract
Whipped cream and chocolate curls or shavings (optional)

1. Heat oven to 300°F.

2. Stir together butter, crumbs, cocoa and sugar in medium bowl; press firmly on bottom of 9-inch springform pan or 13×9-inch baking pan.

3. Place peanut butter chips in small microwave-safe bowl. Microwave at HIGH (100%) 1 minute; stir. If necessary, microwave at HIGH an additional 15 seconds at a time, stirring after each heating, just until chips are melted when stirred. Meanwhile, beat cheese until fluffy. Gradually beat in sweetened condensed milk and melted chips until smooth. Add eggs and vanilla; mix well. Pour into prepared pan.

4. Bake 50 to 60 minutes or until cake springs back when touched lightly. Cool to room temperature. Refrigerate. Garnish with whipped cream and chocolate curls, if desired. Cover; refrigerate leftover cheesecake.

12 servings

PREP TIME: 30 minutes **BAKE TIME:** 50 minutes **COOL TIME:** 1 hour
CHILL TIME: 4 hours

CHOCOLATE TRUFFLE CAKE SUPREME

1¼ cups (2½ sticks) unsalted butter
¾ cup HERSHEY'S Cocoa
1 cup plus 1 tablespoon sugar, divided
1 tablespoon all-purpose flour
2 teaspoons vanilla extract
4 eggs, separated
1 cup (½ pint) cold whipping cream
Chocolate curls (optional)

1. Heat oven to 425°F. Grease bottom of 8-inch springform pan. Melt butter in medium saucepan over low heat. Add cocoa and 1 cup sugar, stir well. Remove from heat; cool. Stir in flour and vanilla. Add egg yolks, one at a time, beating well after each addition. Beat egg whites in medium bowl with remaining 1 tablespoon sugar until soft peaks form; gradually fold into chocolate mixture. Spoon batter into pan.

2. Bake 16 to 18 minutes or until edges are firm (center will be soft). Cool completely on wire rack (cake will sink slightly in center as it cools). Remove side of pan. Refrigerate cake at least 6 hours.

3. Beat whipping cream in small bowl until soft peaks form; spread over top of cake. Cut cake while cold, but let stand at room temperature 10 to 15 minutes before serving. Garnish with chocolate curls, if desired.

10 servings

PREP TIME: 20 minutes **BAKE TIME:** 16 minutes **COOL TIME:** 1 hour
CHILL TIME: 6 hours

CHOCOLATE RASPBERRY POUND CAKE

1 cup seedless black raspberry preserves, divided*
2 cups all-purpose flour
1½ cups granulated sugar
¾ cup HERSHEY'S Cocoa
1½ teaspoons baking soda
1 teaspoon salt
⅔ cup butter or margarine, softened
1 container (16 ounces) dairy sour cream
2 eggs
1 teaspoon vanilla extract
Powdered sugar
RASPBERRY CREAM (recipe follows)

**Red raspberry jam may be substituted.*

1. Heat oven to 350°F. Grease and flour 12-cup fluted tube pan.

2. Place ¾ cup preserves in small microwave-safe bowl. Microwave at HIGH (100%) 30 to 45 seconds or until melted; cool. Stir together flour, granulated sugar, cocoa, baking soda and salt in large bowl. Add butter, sour cream, eggs, vanilla and melted preserves; beat on medium speed of electric mixer 3 to 4 minutes until well blended. Pour batter into prepared pan.

3. Bake 50 to 60 minutes or until wooden pick inserted in center comes out clean. Cool 10 minutes; remove from pan to wire rack. Place remaining ¼ cup preserves in small microwave-safe bowl. Microwave at HIGH 30 seconds or until melted; brush over warm cake. Cool completely.

4. At serving time, sprinkle powdered sugar over top. Prepare RASPBERRY CREAM; fill cavity with cream. Garnish, if desired.

About 12 servings

RASPBERRY CREAM: Thaw 1 package (10 ounces) frozen red raspberries in light syrup. Purée in food processor or blender. Strain into medium bowl; discard seeds. Blend 3½ cups (8 ounces) frozen non-dairy whipped topping, thawed, with raspberry purée. Stir in 2 tablespoons raspberry-flavored liqueur, if desired.

PREP TIME: 35 minutes **BAKE TIME:** 50 minutes **COOL TIME:** 3 hours

Chocolate Raspberry Pound Cake

QUICK 'N' EASY CHOCOLATE CUPCAKES

2 cups all-purpose flour
1½ cups sugar
⅔ cup HERSHEY'S Cocoa
2 teaspoons baking powder
½ teaspoon baking soda
½ teaspoon salt
⅔ cup shortening
2 eggs
⅔ cup milk
½ cup hot water
1½ teaspoons vanilla extract
CREAMY FUDGE FROSTING (recipe follows)

1. Heat oven to 350°F. Line muffin cups (2½ inches in diameter) with paper bake cups.

2. Stir together flour, sugar, cocoa, baking powder, baking soda and salt in large bowl. Add shortening, eggs, milk, water and vanilla; beat on low speed of electric mixer 1 minute. Beat on medium speed an additional 3 minutes or until mixture is smooth. Fill cups ½ full with batter.

3. Bake 15 to 20 minutes or until center of cupcake springs back when touched lightly in center. Remove cupcakes from pan to wire rack. Cool completely. (Do not cool cupcakes in pan; paper liners will come loose from cupcakes.)

4. Prepare CREAMY FUDGE FROSTING; frost cupcakes. Decorate, if desired.

About 30 cupcakes

Creamy Fudge Frosting

½ cup (1 stick) butter or margarine
½ cup HERSHEY'S Cocoa
3⅔ cups (1 pound) powdered sugar
1½ teaspoons vanilla extract
Dash salt
⅓ cup water

Melt butter in medium saucepan over low heat. Add cocoa; stir until smooth and well blended. Remove from heat. Add powdered sugar, vanilla and salt alternately with water; beat with spoon or whisk until smooth and creamy. Additional water may be added, ½ teaspoon at a time, if frosting becomes too thick.

About 2 cups frosting

PREP TIME: 45 minutes **BAKE TIME:** 15 minutes **COOL TIME:** 1 hour

DEEP DARK CHOCOLATE CAKE

2 cups sugar
1¾ cups all-purpose flour
¾ cup HERSHEY'S Cocoa or HERSHEY'S Dutch Processed Cocoa
1½ teaspoons baking powder
1½ teaspoons baking soda
1 teaspoon salt
2 eggs
1 cup milk
½ cup vegetable oil
2 teaspoons vanilla extract
1 cup boiling water
ONE-BOWL BUTTERCREAM FROSTING (recipe follows)

1. Heat oven to 350°F. Grease and flour two 9-inch round baking pans or one 13×9×2-inch baking pan.

2. Stir together sugar, flour, cocoa, baking powder, baking soda and salt in large bowl. Add eggs, milk, oil and vanilla; beat on medium speed of electric mixer 2 minutes. Stir in boiling water (batter will be thin). Pour batter into prepared pans.

3. Bake 30 to 35 minutes for round pans, 35 to 40 minutes for rectangular pan or until wooden pick inserted in center comes out clean. Cool 10 minutes; remove from pans to wire racks. Cool completely. (Cake may be left in rectangular pan, if desired.)

4. Prepare ONE–BOWL BUTTERCREAM FROSTING; frost cake.

8 to 10 servings

One-Bowl Buttercream Frosting

6 tablespoons butter or margarine, softened
2⅔ cups powdered sugar
½ cup HERSHEY'S Cocoa or HERSHEY'S Dutch Processed Cocoa
4 to 6 tablespoons milk
1 teaspoon vanilla extract

Beat butter in medium bowl. Add powdered sugar and cocoa alternately with milk, beating to spreading consistency. Stir in vanilla.

About 2 cups frosting

PREP TIME: 20 minutes **BAKE TIME:** 30 minutes **COOL TIME:** 2 hours

CRUNCHY–TOPPED COCOA CAKE

1½ cups all-purpose flour
1 cup sugar
¼ cup HERSHEY'S Cocoa
1 teaspoon baking soda
½ teaspoon salt
1 cup water
¼ cup plus 2 tablespoons vegetable oil
1 tablespoon white vinegar
1 teaspoon vanilla extract
BROILED TOPPING (recipe follows)

1. Heat oven to 350°F. Grease and flour 8-inch square baking pan.

2. Stir together flour, sugar, cocoa, baking soda and salt in large bowl. Add water, oil, vinegar and vanilla; beat with spoon or whisk just until batter is smooth and ingredients are well blended. Pour batter into prepared pan.

3. Bake 35 to 40 minutes or until wooden pick inserted in center comes out clean. Meanwhile, prepare BROILED TOPPING; spread on warm cake. Set oven to broil; place pan about 4 inches from heat. Broil 3 minutes or until top is bubbly and golden brown. Remove from oven. Cool completely in pan on wire rack. *9 servings*

Broiled Topping

¼ cup (½ stick) butter or margarine, softened
½ cup packed light brown sugar
½ cup coarsely chopped nuts
½ cup MOUNDS Sweetened Coconut Flakes
3 tablespoons light cream or evaporated milk

Stir together all ingredients in small bowl until well blended. *About 1 cup topping*

PREP TIME: 20 minutes **BAKE TIME:** 35 minutes
COOL TIME: 1½ hours

TIP

To make a single serving of "Perfectly Chocolate" Hot Cocoa, stir 2 tablespoons sugar, 2 teaspoons Hershey's Cocoa and a dash of salt in large microwave-safe mug. Gradually add 1 cup hot milk and 1/4 teaspoon vanilla extract, stirring until well blended. Top with miniature marshmallows, if desired.

Crunchy-Topped Cocoa Cake

TAKE–ME–TO–A–PICNIC CAKE

- **1 cup water**
- **1 cup (2 sticks) butter or margarine**
- **½ cup HERSHEY'S Cocoa**
- **2 cups sugar**
- **1¾ cups all-purpose flour**
- **1 teaspoon baking soda**
- **½ teaspoon salt**
- **3 eggs**
- **¾ cup dairy sour cream**
- **PEANUT BUTTER CHIP FROSTING (recipe follows)**
- **CHOCOLATE GARNISH (optional, recipe follows)**

1. Heat oven to 350°F. Grease and flour 15½×10½×1-inch jelly-roll pan. Combine water, butter and cocoa in medium saucepan. Cook over medium heat, stirring occasionally, until mixture boils. Boil 1 minute. Remove from heat. Stir together sugar, flour, baking soda and salt in large bowl. Add eggs and sour cream; beat until blended. Add cocoa mixture; beat just until blended. Pour into prepared pan.

2. Bake 25 to 30 minutes or until wooden pick inserted in center comes out clean. Cool on wire rack. Prepare PEANUT BUTTER CHIP FROSTING. Spread over cake. Prepare CHOCOLATE GARNISH; drizzle over top, if desired. *About 20 servings*

Peanut Butter Chip Frosting: Combine ⅓ cup butter or margarine, ⅓ cup milk and 1⅔ cups (10-ounce package) REESE'S Peanut Butter Chips in medium saucepan. Cook over low heat, stirring constantly, until chips are melted and mixture is smooth. Remove from heat; stir in 1 teaspoon vanilla extract. Place 1 cup powdered sugar in medium bowl. Gradually add chip mixture; beat well. *About 2 cups frosting*

Chocolate Garnish: Place ½ cup HERSHEY'S Semi-Sweet Chocolate Chips and 1 teaspoon shortening (not butter, margarine or oil) in small microwave-safe bowl. Microwave at HIGH (100%) 1 minute; stir until chips are melted and mixture is smooth.

Prep Time: 30 minutes **Bake Time:** 25 minutes **Cool Time:** 1 hour

Take-Me-to-a-Picnic Cake

HOLIDAY CHOCOLATE SHORTBREAD COOKIES

1 cup (2 sticks) butter, softened
1¼ cups powdered sugar
1 teaspoon vanilla extract
½ cup HERSHEY'S Dutch Processed Cocoa or HERSHEY'S Cocoa
1¾ cups all-purpose flour
1⅔ cups (10-ounce package) HERSHEY'S Premier White Chips

1. Heat oven to 300°F. Beat butter, powdered sugar and vanilla in large bowl until creamy. Add cocoa; beat until well blended. Gradually add flour, stirring until smooth.

2. Roll or pat dough to ¼-inch thickness on lightly floured surface or between 2 pieces of wax paper. Cut into holiday shapes using star, tree, wreath or other cookie cutters. Reroll dough scraps, cutting cookies until dough is used. Place on ungreased cookie sheet.

3. Bake 15 to 20 minutes or just until firm. Immediately place white chips, flat side down, in decorative design on warm cookies. Cool slightly; remove from cookie sheet to wire rack. Cool completely. Store in airtight container.

About 4½ dozen (2-inch diameter) cookies

NOTE: For more even baking, place similar shapes and sizes of cookies on same cookie sheet.

PREP TIME: 30 minutes **BAKE TIME:** 15 minutes
COOL TIME: 30 minutes

Holiday Chocolate Shortbread Cookies

HERSHEY'S MINI KISSES PEANUT BLOSSOMS

- ½ cup shortening
- ¾ cup REESE'S Creamy Peanut Butter
- ⅓ cup granulated sugar
- ⅓ cup packed light brown sugar
- 1 egg
- 2 tablespoons milk
- 1 teaspoon vanilla extract
- 1½ cups all-purpose flour
- 1 teaspoon baking soda
- ½ teaspoon salt
- Additional granulated sugar
- 1¾ cups (10-ounce package) HERSHEY'S MINI KISSES Chocolate

1. Heat oven to 375°F. Beat shortening and peanut butter in large bowl until well blended. Add ⅓ cup granulated sugar and brown sugar; beat until light and fluffy. Add egg, milk and vanilla; beat well.

2. Stir together flour, baking soda and salt; gradually add to peanut butter mixture, beating until well blended. Shape dough into 1-inch balls. Roll in additional granulated sugar; place on ungreased cookie sheet.

3. Bake 8 to 10 minutes or until lightly browned. Immediately place 3 MINI KISSES on top of each cookie, pressing down lightly. Remove from cookie sheet to wire rack. Cool completely.

About 4 dozen cookies

PREP TIME: 25 minutes **BAKE TIME:** 8 minutes **COOL TIME:** 1 hour

FUDGEY COCOA NO-BAKE TREATS

- 2 cups sugar
- ½ cup (1 stick) butter or margarine
- ½ cup milk
- ⅓ cup HERSHEY'S Cocoa
- ⅔ cup REESE'S Crunchy Peanut Butter
- 3 cups quick-cooking rolled oats
- ½ cup chopped peanuts (optional)
- 2 teaspoons vanilla extract

1. Place piece of wax paper or foil on tray or cookie sheet. Combine sugar, butter, milk and cocoa in medium saucepan.

2. Cook over medium heat, stirring constantly, until mixture comes to a rolling boil.

3. Remove from heat; cool 1 minute.

4. Add peanut butter, oats, peanuts, if desired, and vanilla; stir to mix well. Quickly drop mixture by heaping teaspoons onto wax paper or foil. Cool completely. Store in cool, dry place. *About 4 dozen*

PREP TIME: 20 minutes **COOK TIME:** 5 minutes **COOL TIME:** 30 minutes

HERSHEY'S MINI KISSES CHOCOLATE BLOSSOMS

1 cup (2 sticks) butter or margarine, softened
1½ cups sugar
2 eggs
2 teaspoons vanilla extract
2 cups all-purpose flour
½ cup HERSHEY'S Cocoa
½ teaspoon salt
Additional sugar
1¾ cups (10-ounce package) HERSHEY'S MINI KISSES Semi-Sweet Chocolate

1. Beat butter, 1½ cups sugar, eggs and vanilla in large bowl until light and fluffy. Stir together flour, cocoa and salt; gradually add to butter mixture, beating until well blended.

2. Refrigerate dough about 1 hour or until firm enough to handle. Heat oven to 350°F. Shape dough into 1⅛-inch balls; roll in additional sugar. Place on ungreased cookie sheet.

3. Bake 8 to 10 minutes or until set. Place 3 MINI KISSES on top of each cookie, pressing down lightly. Remove from cookie sheet to wire rack. Cool completely. *About 4 dozen cookies*

PREP TIME: 25 minutes **CHILL TIME:** 1 hour **BAKE TIME:** 8 minutes
COOL TIME: 1 hour

FUDGEY GERMAN CHOCOLATE SANDWICH COOKIES

1¾ cups all-purpose flour
1½ cups sugar
¾ cup (1½ sticks) butter or margarine, softened
⅔ cup HERSHEY'S Cocoa or HERSHEY'S Dutch Processed Cocoa
¾ teaspoon baking soda
¼ teaspoon salt
2 eggs
2 tablespoons milk
1 teaspoon vanilla extract
½ cup finely chopped pecans
COCONUT AND PECAN FILLING (recipe follows)

1. Heat oven to 350°F. Stir together flour, sugar, butter, cocoa, baking soda and salt in large bowl. Add eggs, milk and vanilla; beat on medium speed of electric mixer until blended. Dough will be stiff. Stir in pecans.

2. Shape dough into 1¼-inch balls. Place on ungreased cookie sheet; flatten slightly.

3. Bake 9 to 11 minutes or until almost set. Cool slightly; remove from cookie sheet to wire rack. Cool completely. Prepare COCONUT AND PECAN FILLING. Put cookies together in pairs with about 1 heaping tablespoon filling for each cookie. Serve warm or at room temperature.

About 17 sandwich cookies

Coconut and Pecan Filling

½ cup (1 stick) butter or margarine
½ cup packed light brown sugar
¼ cup light corn syrup
1 cup MOUNDS Sweetened Coconut Flakes, toasted
1 cup finely chopped pecans
1 teaspoon vanilla extract

Melt butter in medium saucepan over medium heat; add brown sugar and corn syrup. Stir constantly until thick and bubbly. Remove from heat; stir in coconut, pecans and vanilla. Use warm. *About 2 cups filling*

PREP TIME: 25 minutes **BAKE TIME:** 9 minutes **COOL TIME:** 35 minutes

Fudgey German Chocolate Sandwich Cookies

CHOCOLATE ALMOND BISCOTTI

- **½ cup (1 stick) butter or margarine, softened**
- **1¼ cups sugar**
- **2 eggs**
- **1 teaspoon almond extract**
- **2¼ cups all-purpose flour**
- **¼ cup HERSHEY'S Dutch Processed Cocoa or HERSHEY'S Cocoa**
- **1 teaspoon baking powder**
- **¼ teaspoon salt**
- **1 cup sliced almonds**
- **CHOCOLATE GLAZE (recipe follows)**
- **WHITE GLAZE (recipe follows)**
- **Additional sliced almonds (optional)**

1. Heat oven to 350°F. Beat butter and sugar until blended. Add eggs and almond extract; beat well. Stir together flour, cocoa, baking powder and salt; gradually add to butter mixture, beating until smooth. (Dough will be thick.) Stir in almonds using wooden spoon.

2. Shape dough into two 11-inch-long rolls. Place rolls 3 to 4 inches apart on large ungreased cookie sheet.

3. Bake 30 minutes or until rolls are set. Remove from oven; cool on cookie sheet 15 minutes. Using serrated knife, cut rolls diagonally using sawing motion, into ½-inch-thick slices. Arrange slices, cut sides down, close together on cookie sheet.

4. Bake 8 to 9 minutes. Turn slices over; bake an additional 8 to 9 minutes. Remove from oven; cool on cookie sheet on wire rack. Prepare CHOCOLATE GLAZE. Dip end of each biscotti in glaze or drizzle over entire cookie. Prepare WHITE GLAZE; drizzle over chocolate glaze. Garnish with additional almonds, if desired. *About 2½ dozen cookies*

CHOCOLATE GLAZE: Place 1 cup HERSHEY'S Semi-Sweet Chocolate Chips and 1 tablespoon shortening (do not use butter, margarine or oil) into small microwave-safe bowl. Microwave at HIGH (100%) 1 to 1½ minutes or until smooth when stirred. *About 1 cup glaze*

WHITE GLAZE: Place ¼ cup HERSHEY'S Premier White Chips and 1 teaspoon shortening (do not use butter, margarine or oil) into small microwave-safe bowl. Microwave at HIGH (100%) 30 to 45 seconds or until smooth when stirred. *About ¼ cup glaze*

PREP TIME: 30 minutes **BAKE TIME:** 46 minutes **COOL TIME:** 1 hour

Chocolate Almond Biscotti

NO–BAKE BUTTERSCOTCH HAYSTACKS

1 cup HERSHEY'S Butterscotch Chips
½ cup REESE'S Peanut Butter Chips
1 tablespoon shortening (do not use butter, margarine or oil)
1½ cups (3-ounce can) chow mein noodles, coarsely broken

1. Line cookie sheet with wax paper. Place butterscotch chips, peanut butter chips and shortening in medium microwave-safe bowl.

2. Microwave at HIGH (100%) 1 minute; stir. If necessary, microwave at HIGH an additional 15 seconds at a time, stirring after each heating, just until chips are melted and mixture is smooth when stirred.

3. Immediately add chow mein noodles; stir to coat. Drop mixture by heaping teaspoons onto prepared cookie sheet or into paper candy cups; let stand until firm. If necessary, cover and refrigerate until firm. Store in refrigerator in tightly covered container. *About 2 dozen cookies*

Chocolate Haystacks: Substitute 1 cup HERSHEY'S Semi-Sweet Chocolate Chips or HERSHEY'S Milk Chocolate Chips for butterscotch chips. Proceed as directed above with peanut butter chips, shortening and chow mein noodles.

Prep Time: 15 minutes **Cook Time:** 1 minute **Cool Time:** 30 minutes

HERSHEY'S CHOCOLATETOWN CHIP COOKIES

1 cup shortening OR ¾ cup (1½ sticks) butter or margarine
1 cup packed light brown sugar
½ cup granulated sugar
1 teaspoon vanilla extract
2 eggs
2¼ cups all-purpose flour
1 teaspoon baking soda
1 teaspoon salt
2 cups (11.5-ounce package) HERSHEY'S Milk Chocolate Chips
1 cup chopped nuts (optional)

1. Heat oven to 375°F. Beat shortening, brown sugar, granulated sugar and vanilla in large bowl until light and fluffy. Add eggs; beat well.

2. Stir together flour, baking soda and salt; add to beaten mixture, stirring until well blended. Stir in chips and nuts, if desired. Drop by teaspoons onto ungreased cookie sheet.

3. Bake 8 to 10 minutes or until lightly browned. Cool slightly; remove from cookie sheet to wire rack. Cool completely.

About 5 dozen cookies

PREP TIME: 25 minutes **BAKE TIME:** 8 minutes **COOL TIME:** 35 minutes

SKOR BITS & CHOCOLATE CHIP COOKIES

2¼ cups all-purpose flour
1 teaspoon baking soda
½ teaspoon salt
¾ cup (1½ sticks) butter or margarine, softened
¾ cup granulated sugar
¾ cup packed light brown sugar
1 teaspoon vanilla extract
2 eggs
1 cup SKOR English Toffee Bits or 1 cup HEATH Bits 'O Brickle
1 cup HERSHEY'S Semi-Sweet Chocolate Chips

1. Heat oven to 375°F. Stir together flour, baking soda and salt. Beat butter, granulated sugar, brown sugar and vanilla in large bowl until well blended. Add eggs; beat well.

2. Gradually add flour mixture, beating well. Stir in toffee bits and chocolate chips. Drop dough by rounded teaspoons onto ungreased cookie sheet.

3. Bake 8 to 10 minutes or until lightly browned. Cool slightly; remove from cookie sheet to wire rack. Cool completely.

About 4 dozen cookies

PREP TIME: 25 minutes **BAKE TIME:** 8 minutes **COOL TIME:** 30 minutes

HOLIDAY BITS CUTOUT COOKIES

> ***TIP***
>
> *Brownies, bars and cookies make great gifts. Place them in a paper-lined tin or on a decorative plate covered with plastic wrap and tied with colorful ribbon. For a special touch, include the recipe.*

1 cup (2 sticks) butter or margarine, softened
1 cup sugar
2 eggs
2 teaspoons vanilla extract
2½ cups all-purpose flour
½ teaspoon baking powder
½ teaspoon salt
HERSHEY'S Holiday Candy Coated Bits

1. Beat butter, sugar, eggs and vanilla in large bowl on low speed of electric mixer just until blended. Stir together flour, baking powder and salt; add to butter mixture, stirring until well blended.

2. Divide dough in half. Cover; refrigerate 1 to 2 hours or until firm enough to handle. Heat oven to 400°F. On lightly floured surface, roll each half of the dough to about ¼ inch thick.

3. Cut into tree, wreath, star or other shapes with 2½-inch cookie cutters. Place on ungreased cookie sheet. Press candy coated bits into cutouts.

4. Bake 6 to 8 minutes or until edges are firm and bottoms are very lightly browned. Remove from cookie sheet to wire rack. Cool completely. *About 3½ dozen cookies*

PREP TIME: 30 minutes **CHILL TIME:** 1 hour
BAKE TIME: 6 minutes

Holiday Bits Cutout Cookies

CHEWY CHOCOLATE MACAROONS

5⅓ cups MOUNDS Sweetened Coconut Flakes
½ cup HERSHEY'S Cocoa
1 can (14 ounces) sweetened condensed milk (not evaporated milk)
2 teaspoons vanilla extract
About 24 red candied cherries, halved (optional)

1. Heat oven to 350°F. Generously grease cookie sheet. Stir together coconut and cocoa in large bowl; stir in sweetened condensed milk and vanilla until well blended. Drop by rounded teaspoons onto prepared cookie sheet. Press cherry half into center of each cookie, if desired.

2. Bake 8 to 10 minutes or until almost set. Immediately remove from cookie sheet to wire rack. Cool completely. Store loosely covered at room temperature. *About 4 dozen cookies*

PREP TIME: 15 minutes **BAKE TIME:** 8 minutes **COOL TIME:** 1 hour

CHEWY SKOR TOFFEE BITS COOKIES

2¼ cups all-purpose flour
1 teaspoon baking soda
½ teaspoon salt
½ cup (1 stick) butter or margarine, softened
¾ cup granulated sugar
¾ cup packed light brown sugar
1 teaspoon vanilla extract
2 eggs
1¾ cups (10-ounce package) SKOR English Toffee Bits or 1¾ cups HEATH Bits O' Brickle

1. Heat oven to 350°F. Lightly grease cookie sheet.

2. Stir together flour, baking soda and salt. Beat butter, granulated sugar, brown sugar and vanilla in large bowl until well blended. Add eggs; beat well. Gradually add flour mixture, beating until well blended. Stir in toffee bits. Drop by rounded teaspoons onto prepared cookie sheet.

3. Bake 9 to 11 minutes or until lightly browned. Cool slightly; remove from cookie sheet to wire rack. Cool completely.

About 4 dozen cookies

PREP TIME: 25 minutes **COOK TIME:** 9 minutes **COOL TIME:** 1 hour

Chewy Chocolate Macaroons

FOURTH

MINI KISSES COCONUT MACAROON BARS

3¾ cups (10-ounce package) MOUNDS Sweetened Coconut Flakes
¾ cup sugar
¼ cup all-purpose flour
¼ teaspoon salt
3 egg whites
1 whole egg, slightly beaten
1 teaspoon almond extract
1 cup HERSHEY'S MINI KISSES Chocolate

1. Heat oven to 350°F. Lightly grease 9-inch square baking pan. Stir together coconut, sugar, flour and salt in large bowl. Add egg whites, whole egg and almond extract; stir until well blended.

2. Stir in MINI KISSES. Spread mixture into prepared pan, covering all chocolate pieces with coconut mixture.

3. Bake 35 minutes or until lightly browned. Cool completely in pan on wire rack. Cover with foil; allow to stand at room temperature about 8 hours or overnight. Cut into bars. *About 24 bars*

VARIATION: Omit MINI KISSES in batter. Immediately after removing pan from oven, place desired number of chocolate pieces on top, pressing down lightly. Cool completely. Cut into bars.

PREP TIME: 15 minutes **BAKE TIME:** 35 minutes
COOL TIME: 9 hours

Mini Kisses Coconut Macaroon Bars

PECAN MINI KISSES CUPS

Tip

Use MINI KISSES Chocolate to decorate cakes, cupcakes, cookies and pies. Stir into slightly softened ice cream or sprinkle over top of a sundae for an added chocolate taste treat.

½ cup (1 stick) butter or margarine, softened
1 package (3 ounces) cream cheese, softened
1 cup all-purpose flour
1 egg
⅔ cup packed light brown sugar
1 tablespoon butter, melted
1 teaspoon vanilla extract
Dash salt
72 HERSHEY'S MINI KISSES Chocolate, divided
½ to ¾ cup coarsely chopped pecans

1. Beat ½ cup softened butter and cream cheese in medium bowl until blended. Add flour; beat well. Cover; refrigerate about 1 hour or until firm enough to handle.

2. Heat oven to 325°F. Stir together egg, brown sugar, 1 tablespoon melted butter, vanilla and salt in small bowl until well blended.

3. Shape chilled dough into 24 balls (1 inch each). Place balls in ungreased small muffin cups (1¾ inches in diameter). Press onto bottom and up side of cups. Place 2 MINI KISSES in each cup. Spoon about 1 teaspoon pecans over chocolate. Fill each cup with egg mixture.

4. Bake 25 minutes or until filling is set. Lightly press 1 MINI KISS into center of each cookie. Cool in pan on wire rack.

24 cups

Prep Time: 25 minutes **Chill Time:** 1 hour
Bake Time: 25 minutes **Cool Time:** 1 hour

Pecan Mini Kisses Cups

RICH QUICK & EASY CHOCOLATE BROWNIES

½ cup sugar
¼ cup evaporated milk
¼ cup (½ stick) butter or margarine
8 bars (8-ounce package) HERSHEY'S Semi-Sweet Baking Chocolate, broken into pieces
2 eggs
1 teaspoon vanilla extract
¾ cup all-purpose flour
¼ teaspoon baking soda
¼ teaspoon salt
BROWNIE FROSTING (recipe follows, optional)

1. Heat oven to 325°F. Grease 9-inch square baking pan. Combine sugar, evaporated milk and butter in medium saucepan.

2. Cook over medium heat, stirring constantly, until mixture boils; remove from heat. Add chocolate, stirring until melted. Beat in eggs and vanilla. Stir in flour, baking soda and salt until well blended; pour into prepared pan.

3. Bake 30 to 35 minutes or until brownies just begin to pull away from sides of pan. Cool completely in pan on wire rack. Prepare BROWNIE FROSTING; frost brownies, if desired. Cut into squares.

About 16 brownies

Brownie Frosting

2 bars (1 ounce each) HERSHEY'S Unsweetened Baking Chocolate, broken into pieces
2 tablespoons butter or margarine
1¾ cups powdered sugar
⅛ teaspoon salt
½ teaspoon vanilla extract
2 to 3 tablespoons water

Place chocolate and butter in small microwave-safe bowl. Microwave at HIGH (100%) 1 minute; stir. If necessary, microwave an additional 10 seconds at a time, stirring after each heating, just until chocolate is melted when stirred. Combine powdered sugar and salt in medium bowl. Stir in chocolate mixture and vanilla. Add water; beat with spoon to spreading consistency.

About 1 cup frosting

PREP TIME: 30 minutes **BAKE TIME:** 30 minutes **COOL TIME:** 2 hours

ULTIMATE CHOCOLATE BROWNIES WITH CREAMY COCOA FROSTING

¾ cup HERSHEY'S Cocoa
½ teaspoon baking soda
⅔ cup butter or margarine, melted and divided
½ cup boiling water
2 cups sugar
2 eggs
1⅓ cups all-purpose flour
1 teaspoon vanilla extract
¼ teaspoon salt
1 cup HERSHEY'S Semi-Sweet Chocolate Chips
CREAMY COCOA FROSTING (recipe follows)

1. Heat oven to 350°F. Grease 13×9×2-inch baking pan. Stir together cocoa and baking soda in large bowl; stir in ⅓ cup butter. Add boiling water; stir until mixture thickens.

2. Stir in sugar, eggs and remaining ⅓ cup butter; stir until smooth. Add flour, vanilla and salt; stir until blended. Stir in chocolate chips. Pour into prepared pan.

3. Bake 35 to 40 minutes or until brownies begin to pull away from sides of pan. Cool completely.

4. Prepare CREAMY COCOA FROSTING; frost brownies. Garnish with additional chips, if desired. Cut into squares. *About 36 brownies*

Creamy Cocoa Frosting

6 tablespoons butter or margarine, softened
2⅔ cups powdered sugar
½ cup HERSHEY'S Cocoa
¼ cup milk
1 tablespoon espresso powder dissolved in 1 tablespoon hot water
½ teaspoon vanilla extract

Beat butter in medium bowl. Add powdered sugar and cocoa alternately with milk, espresso and vanilla, beating to spreading consistency.
About 2 cups frosting

PREP TIME: 30 minutes **BAKE TIME:** 35 minutes **COOL TIME:** 2 hours

HERSHEY'S WHITE CHIP BROWNIES

Tip

Brownies and bar cookies cut into different shapes can add interest to a plate of simple square cookies. Cut cookies into different size rectangles or make triangles by cutting them into 2- to 2½-inch squares; cut each square in half diagonally. To make diamond shapes, cut straight lines 1 or 1½ inches apart the length of the baking pan, then cut straight lines 1½ inches apart diagonally across the pan.

4 eggs
1¼ cups sugar
½ cup (1 stick) butter or margarine, melted
2 teaspoons vanilla extract
1⅓ cups all-purpose flour
⅔ cup HERSHEY'S Cocoa
1 teaspoon baking powder
½ teaspoon salt
1⅔ cups (10-ounce package) HERSHEY'S Premier White Chips

1. Heat oven to 350°F. Grease 13×9×2-inch baking pan. Beat eggs in large bowl until foamy; gradually beat in sugar. Add butter and vanilla; beat until blended.

2. Stir together flour, cocoa, baking powder and salt; add to egg mixture, beating until blended. Stir in white chips. Spread batter into prepared pan.

3. Bake 25 to 30 minutes or until brownies begin to pull away from sides of pan. Cool completely in pan on wire rack. Cut into squares. *About 36 brownies*

PREP TIME: 15 minutes **BAKE TIME:** 25 minutes
COOL TIME: 2 hours

Hershey's White Chip Brownies

PEANUT BUTTER CHIP TRIANGLES

> ### *Tip*
> *To sprinkle powdered sugar over brownies, bars, cupcakes or other desserts, place sugar in a wire mesh strainer. Hold over top of desserts and gently tap sides of strainer.*

1½ cups all-purpose flour
½ cup packed light brown sugar
½ cup (1 stick) cold butter or margarine
1⅔ cups (10-ounce package) REESE'S Peanut Butter Chips, divided
1 can (14 ounces) sweetened condensed milk (not evaporated milk)
1 egg, slightly beaten
1 teaspoon vanilla extract
¾ cup chopped walnuts
Powdered sugar (optional)

1. Heat oven to 350°F. Stir together flour and brown sugar in medium bowl. Cut in butter with pastry blender or fork until mixture resembles coarse crumbs. Stir in ½ cup peanut butter chips. Press mixture into bottom of ungreased 13×9×2-inch baking pan. Bake 15 minutes.

2. Meanwhile, in large bowl, combine sweetened condensed milk, egg and vanilla. Stir in remaining chips and walnuts. Spread evenly over hot baked crust.

3. Bake 25 minutes or until golden brown. Cool completely in pan on wire rack. Cut into 2- or 2½-inch squares; cut squares diagonally into triangles. Sift powdered sugar over top, if desired. *24 or 40 triangles*

Prep Time: 20 minutes **Bake Time:** 40 minutes
Cool Time: 2 hours

Peanut Butter Chip Triangles

MARBLED CHEESECAKE BARS

CHOCOLATE CRUST (recipe follows)
3 packages (8 ounces each) cream cheese, softened
1 can (14 ounces) sweetened condensed milk (not evaporated milk)
3 eggs
2 teaspoons vanilla extract
2 bars (1 ounce each) HERSHEY'S Unsweetened Baking Chocolate, melted

1. Prepare CHOCOLATE CRUST. Heat oven to 300°F. Beat cream cheese in large bowl until fluffy. Gradually add sweetened condensed milk, beating until smooth. Add eggs and vanilla; mix well.

2. Pour half of batter evenly over prepared crust. Stir melted chocolate into remaining batter; drop by spoonfuls over vanilla batter. With metal spatula or knife, swirl gently through batter to marble.

3. Bake 45 to 50 minutes or until set. Cool in pan on wire rack. Refrigerate several hours until chilled. Cut into bars. Cover; store leftover bars in refrigerator. *24 to 36 bars*

CHOCOLATE CRUST: Stir together 2 cups vanilla wafer crumbs (about 60 wafers), ⅓ cup HERSHEY'S Cocoa and ½ cup powdered sugar. Stir in ½ cup (1 stick) melted butter or margarine until well blended. Press mixture firmly into bottom of ungreased 13×9×2-inch baking pan.

PREP TIME: 25 minutes **BAKE TIME:** 45 minutes **COOL TIME:** 1 hour
CHILL TIME: 2½ hours

NUTTY CHOCOLATE BROWNIES

8 bars (8-ounce package) HERSHEY'S Bittersweet Baking Chocolate, broken into pieces
1 cup (2 sticks) butter or margarine
1¼ cups sugar
3 eggs
2 teaspoons vanilla extract
1½ teaspoons powdered instant coffee
1⅓ cups all-purpose flour
½ teaspoon salt
¼ teaspoon baking powder
¼ teaspoon baking soda
1 cup coarsely chopped nuts

1. Heat oven to 350°F. Grease 13×9×2-inch baking pan. Combine chocolate and butter in medium saucepan. Cook over medium heat, stirring constantly, until melted.

2. Remove from heat; stir in sugar. Add eggs, one at a time, stirring well after each addition. Stir in vanilla and instant coffee until blended. Combine flour, salt, baking powder, baking soda and nuts; add to chocolate mixture, stirring until well blended. Spread batter into prepared pan.

3. Bake 25 to 30 minutes or until wooden pick inserted in center comes out almost clean. Cool completely in pan on wire rack. Cut into squares.

About 36 brownies

PREP TIME: 25 minutes **BAKE TIME:** 25 minutes **COOL TIME:** 2 hours

MINI KISSES COOKIE BARS

- **½ cup (1 stick) butter or margarine, softened**
- **½ cup shortening**
- **1 cup packed light brown sugar**
- **½ cup granulated sugar**
- **2 eggs**
- **1 teaspoon vanilla extract**
- **½ teaspoon baking soda**
- **2½ cups all-purpose flour**
- **1¾ cups (10-ounce package) HERSHEY'S MINI KISSES Chocolate, divided**
- **1 cup chopped nuts (optional)**

1. Heat oven to 375°F. Beat butter and shortening in large bowl on medium speed of mixer just until blended.

2. Add brown sugar and granulated sugar; beat well. Beat in eggs, vanilla and baking soda. Gradually beat in flour (if dough becomes too stiff, stir in remaining flour with spoon). Set aside ½ cup MINI KISSES; stir in remaining MINI KISSES and nuts, if desired. Press dough into ungreased 15½×10½×1-inch jelly-roll pan.

3. Bake 15 to 20 minutes or until top is golden. Remove from oven; immediately place reserved MINI KISSES on top, pressing down lightly. Cool completely in pan on wire rack. Cut into bars. *About 48 bars*

PREP TIME: 20 minutes **BAKE TIME:** 15 minutes **COOL TIME:** 2 hours

MARBLED CHERRY BROWNIES

CHERRY CREAM FILLING (recipe follows)
½ cup (1 stick) butter or margarine, melted
⅓ cup HERSHEY'S Cocoa
2 eggs
1 cup sugar
1 teaspoon vanilla extract
½ cup all-purpose flour
½ teaspoon baking powder
¼ teaspoon salt

1. Prepare CHERRY CREAM FILLING; set aside. Heat oven to 350°F. Grease 9-inch square baking pan. Stir butter and cocoa in small bowl until well blended; cool slightly.

2. Beat eggs in medium bowl until foamy. Gradually add sugar and vanilla, beating until well blended. Stir together flour, baking powder and salt; add to egg mixture. Add cocoa mixture; stir until well blended.

3. Spread half of chocolate batter into prepared pan; cover with cherry filling. Drop spoonfuls of remaining chocolate batter over filling. With knife or spatula, gently swirl chocolate batter into filling for marbled effect.

4. Bake 35 to 40 minutes or until brownies begin to pull away from sides of pan. Cool; cut into squares. Cover; refrigerate leftover brownies. Bring to room temperature to serve. *About 16 brownies*

Cherry Cream Filling

1 package (3 ounces) cream cheese, softened,
¼ cup sugar
1 egg
½ teaspoon vanilla extract
¼ teaspoon almond extract
⅓ cup chopped maraschino cherries, well drained
1 to 2 drops red food color (optional)

1. Beat cream cheese and sugar in small bowl on medium speed of electric mixer until blended. Add egg, vanilla and almond extract; beat well. (Mixture will be thin.)

2. Stir in cherries and food color, if desired.

PREP TIME: 25 minutes **BAKE TIME:** 35 minutes **COOL TIME:** 1½ hours

Marbled Cherry Brownies

CREAMY DOUBLE DECKER FUDGE

- **1 cup REESE'S Peanut Butter Chips**
- **1 can (14 ounces) sweetened condensed milk (not evaporated milk), divided**
- **1 teaspoon vanilla extract, divided**
- **1 cup HERSHEY'S Semi-Sweet Chocolate Chips**

1. Line 8-inch square pan with foil, extending foil over edges of pan. Place peanut butter chips and ⅔ cup sweetened condensed milk in small microwave-safe bowl.

2. Microwave at HIGH (100%) 1 to 1½ minutes, stirring after 1 minute, until chips are melted and mixture is smooth when stirred. Stir in ½ teaspoon vanilla; spread evenly into prepared pan.

3. Place remaining sweetened condensed milk and chocolate chips in another small microwave-safe bowl; repeat above microwave procedure. Stir in remaining ½ teaspoon vanilla; spread evenly over peanut butter layer. Cover; refrigerate until firm. Remove from pan; place on cutting board. Peel off foil. Cut into squares. Store, tightly covered, in refrigerator.

About 4 dozen pieces or 1½ pounds

NOTE: For best results, do not double this recipe.

PREP TIME: 15 minutes **COOK TIME:** 3 minutes
CHILL TIME: 2 hours

Creamy Double Decker Fudge

RICH COCOA FUDGE

3 cups sugar
2/3 cup HERSHEY'S Cocoa or HERSHEY'S Dutch Processed Cocoa
1/8 teaspoon salt
1 1/2 cups milk
1/4 cup (1/2 stick) butter
1 teaspoon vanilla extract

1. Line 8- or 9-inch square pan with foil, extending foil over edges of pan. Butter foil.

2. Stir together sugar, cocoa and salt in heavy 4-quart saucepan; stir in milk. Cook over medium heat, stirring constantly, until mixture comes to full rolling boil. Boil, without stirring, until mixture reaches 234°F on candy thermometer or until small amount of mixture dropped into very cold water, forms a soft ball which flattens when removed from water. (Bulb of candy thermometer should not rest on bottom of saucepan.) Remove from heat.

3. Add butter and vanilla. DO NOT STIR. Cool at room temperature to 110°F (lukewarm). Beat with wooden spoon until fudge thickens and just begins to lose some of its gloss. Quickly spread into prepared pan; cool completely. Cut into squares. Store in tightly covered container at room temperature. *About 3 dozen pieces or 1 3/4 pounds*

NOTE: For best results, do not double this recipe.

NUTTY RICH COCOA FUDGE: Beat cooked fudge as directed. Immediately stir in 1 cup chopped almonds, pecans or walnuts and quickly spread into prepared pan.

MARSHMALLOW-NUT COCOA FUDGE: Increase cocoa to 3/4 cup. Cook fudge as directed. Add 1 cup marshmallow creme with butter and vanilla. DO NOT STIR. Cool to 110°F (lukewarm). Beat 8 minutes; stir in 1 cup chopped nuts. Pour into prepared pan. (Fudge does not set until poured into pan.)

PREP TIME: 25 minutes **COOK TIME:** 25 minutes **COOL TIME:** 2 1/2 hours

CHOCOLATE PEANUT CLUSTERS

½ cup HERSHEY'S Milk Chocolate Chips
½ cup HERSHEY'S Semi-Sweet Chocolate Chips
1 tablespoon shortening (do not use butter, margarine or oil)
1 cup unsalted, roasted peanuts

1. Place milk chocolate chips, semi-sweet chocolate chips and shortening in small microwave-safe bowl. Microwave at HIGH (100%) 1 to 1½ minutes or just until chips are melted and mixture is smooth when stirred. Stir in peanuts.

2. Drop by teaspoons into 1-inch diameter candy or petit four papers. Allow to set until firm. Store in airtight container in cool, dry place.

About 2 dozen candies

PREP TIME: 15 minutes **COOK TIME:** 1 minute **COOL TIME:** 1 hour

FOOLPROOF DARK CHOCOLATE FUDGE

3 cups (1½ packages, 12-ounces each) HERSHEY'S Semi-Sweet Chocolate Chips
1 can (14 ounces) sweetened condensed milk (not evaporated milk)
Dash salt
1 cup chopped walnuts
1½ teaspoons vanilla extract

1. Line 8- or 9-inch square pan with foil, extending foil over edges of pan. Melt chocolate chips with sweetened condensed milk and salt in heavy saucepan over low heat. Remove from heat; stir in walnuts and vanilla. Spread evenly into prepared pan.

2. Refrigerate 2 hours or until firm. Remove from pan; place on cutting board. Peel off foil; cut into squares. Store loosely covered at room temperature.

About 5 dozen pieces or 2 pounds

NOTE: For best results, do not double this recipe.

PREP TIME: 10 minutes **COOK TIME:** 15 minutes **CHILL TIME:** 2 hours

CASHEW MACADAMIA CRUNCH

2 cups (11.5 ounce package) HERSHEY'S Milk Chocolate Chips
¾ cup coarsely chopped salted or unsalted cashews
¾ cup coarsely chopped salted or unsalted macadamia nuts
½ cup (1 stick) butter, softened
½ cup sugar
2 tablespoons light corn syrup

1. Line 9-inch square pan with foil, extending foil over edges of pan. Butter foil. Cover bottom of prepared pan with chocolate chips.

2. Combine cashews, macadamia nuts, butter, sugar and corn syrup in large heavy skillet; cook over low heat, stirring constantly, until butter is melted and sugar is dissolved. Increase heat to medium; cook, stirring constantly, until mixture begins to cling together and turns golden brown.

3. Pour mixture over chocolate chips in pan, spreading evenly. Cool. Refrigerate until chocolate is firm. Remove from pan; peel off foil. Break into pieces. Store, tightly covered in cool, dry place. *About 1½ pounds*

PREP TIME: 30 minutes **COOK TIME:** 10 minutes **COOL TIME:** 40 minutes
CHILL TIME: 3 hours

CHOCOLATE & PEANUT BUTTER TRUFFLES

¾ cup (1½ sticks) butter (no substitutes)
1 cup REESE'S Peanut Butter Chips
½ cup HERSHEY'S Cocoa
1 can (14 ounces) sweetened condensed milk (not evaporated milk)
1 tablespoon vanilla extract
HERSHEY'S Cocoa or finely chopped nuts or graham cracker crumbs

1. Melt butter and peanut butter chips in saucepan over very low heat. Add cocoa; stir until smooth. Add sweetened condensed milk; stir constantly until mixture is thick and glossy, about 4 minutes. Remove from heat; stir in vanilla.

2. Refrigerate 2 hours or until firm enough to handle. Shape into 1-inch balls; roll in cocoa. Refrigerate until firm, about 1 hour. Store, covered, in refrigerator. *About 3½ dozen candies*

PREP TIME: 30 minutes **COOK TIME:** 7 minutes **CHILL TIME:** 3 hours

Cashew Macadamia Crunch

OLD–FASHIONED CREAMY FUDGE

2 cups sugar
¾ cup milk
2½ bars (1 ounce each) HERSHEY'S Unsweetened Baking Chocolate, broken into pieces
2 tablespoons light corn syrup
¼ teaspoon salt
2 tablespoons butter
1 teaspoon vanilla extract

1. Line 8-inch square pan with foil, extending foil over edges of pan. Lightly butter foil.

2. Stir together sugar, milk, baking chocolate, corn syrup and salt in heavy 2-quart saucepan. Cook over medium heat, stirring constantly, until mixture comes to full rolling boil. Cook, stirring occasionally, until mixture reaches 234°F on candy thermometer or until small amount of mixture dropped into very cold water forms a soft ball, which flattens when removed from water. (Bulb of candy thermometer should not rest on bottom of saucepan.)

3. Remove from heat. Add butter and vanilla. DO NOT STIR. Cool at room temperature to 110°F (lukewarm). Beat with wooden spoon until fudge thickens and just begins to lose some of its gloss. Quickly spread into prepared pan. Cool completely. Cut into squares. Store in tightly covered container at room temperature.

About 3 dozen pieces or 1½ pounds

NOTE: For best results, do not double this recipe.

PREP TIME: 20 minutes **COOK TIME:** 25 minutes **COOL TIME:** 2½ hours

WHITE COATED CHOCOLATE TRUFFLES

½ cup whipping cream
3 tablespoons butter
1 cup HERSHEY'S Semi-Sweet Chocolate Chips
1 teaspoon vanilla extract
WHITE COATING (page 59)

1. Combine whipping cream and butter in medium saucepan. Cook over medium heat, stirring constantly, just until mixture begins to boil; remove from heat. Add chocolate chips, stirring until completely melted;

continue stirring until mixture cools and thickens slightly. Stir in vanilla. Pour into shallow, glass dish. Cover; refrigerate until firm.

2. To form truffles, with spoon, scoop mixture; shape into 1-inch balls. Place on wax paper-lined tray. Cover; refrigerate until firm. Prepare WHITE COATING. Dip truffles into coating; refrigerate. Serve well chilled. Store in tightly covered container in refrigerator.

About 2 dozen truffles

WHITE COATING: Combine 1⅔ cups (10-ounce package) HERSHEY'S Premier White Chips with 1 tablespoon shortening (do not use butter, margarine or oil) in small microwave-safe bowl. Microwave at HIGH (100%) 1 minute or just until chips are melted when stirred. (Coating works best for dipping between 85° and 90°F. If coating goes below 85°F, place bowl in larger bowl containing warm water; stir until temperature reaches 85°F. Be careful not to get any water into coating mixture.)

PREP TIME: 1 hour **COOK TIME:** 3 minutes **COOL TIME:** 10 minutes
CHILL TIME: 5 hours

CHOCOLATE CHIP PEANUT BUTTER FUDGE

4 cups sugar
1 jar (7 ounces) marshmallow creme
1½ cups (12-ounce can) evaporated milk
1 cup REESE'S Creamy or Crunchy Peanut Butter
1 tablespoon butter or margarine
1 cup HERSHEY'S Semi-Sweet Chocolate Chips or HERSHEY'S Milk Chocolate Chips

1. Line 13×9×2-inch pan with foil, extending foil over edges of pan. Lightly butter foil.

2. Stir together sugar, marshmallow creme, evaporated milk, peanut butter and butter in heavy 4-quart saucepan. Cook over medium heat, stirring constantly, until mixture comes to full rolling boil; boil and stir 5 minutes. Remove from heat. Immediately add chocolate chips, stir until smooth. Pour into prepared pan; cool until firm.

3. Use foil to lift fudge out of pan; peel off foil. Cut fudge into squares. Store in tightly covered container in cool, dry place.

About 8 dozen pieces or 3½ pounds

NOTE: For best results, do not double this recipe.

PREP TIME: 15 minutes **COOK TIME:** 15 minutes **COOL TIME:** 3 hours

CHOCOLATE–COVERED ALMOND APRICOT TASSIES

TIP

When melting chocolate, even a small amount of moisture my cause it to "seize" or become stiff and grainy. Chocolate can sometimes be returned to melting consistency by adding 1 teaspoon solid shortening (do not use butter, margarine or oil) for every 2 ounces of chocolate and reheating it.

2 cups vanilla wafer crumbs (about 60 wafers, crushed)
1 cup finely chopped almonds
⅓ cup HERSHEY'S Cocoa
1 can (14 ounces) sweetened condensed milk (not evaporated milk)
1 package (8 ounces) dried apricots, chopped
½ cup chopped candied cherries
¼ teaspoon almond extract
2 cups (11.5-ounce package) HERSHEY'S Milk Chocolate Chips
4 teaspoons shortening

1. Line small muffin cups (1¾ inches in diameter) with paper bake cups.

2. Combine crumbs, almonds and cocoa in large bowl. Add sweetened condensed milk, apricots, cherries and almond extract; mix well. Refrigerate 30 minutes. Roll mixture into 1-inch balls; press into prepared muffin cups.

3. Place chocolate chips and shortening in medium microwave-safe bowl. Microwave at HIGH (100%) 1½ minutes; stir. If necessary, microwave at HIGH an additional 15 seconds at a time, stirring after each heating, just until chips are melted when stirred. Spoon about 1 teaspoon melted chocolate over each filled cup. Refrigerate until chocolate is set. Store, covered, in refrigerator.

About 6 dozen candies

PREP TIME: 40 minutes **COOK TIME:** 1½ minutes
CHILL TIME: 1 hour

Chocolate-Covered Almond Apricot Tassies

CHOCOLATE COCONUT BALLS

- **3 bars (1 ounce each) HERSHEY'S Unsweetened Baking Chocolate**
- **¼ cup (½ stick) butter**
- **½ cup sweetened condensed milk (not evaporated milk)**
- **¾ cup granulated sugar**
- **¼ cup water**
- **1 tablespoon light corn syrup**
- **1 teaspoon vanilla extract**
- **2 cups MOUNDS Sweetened Coconut Flakes**
- **1 cup chopped nuts**
- **Powdered sugar**

1. Melt chocolate and butter in large heavy saucepan over very low heat. Add sweetened condensed milk; stir to blend. Remove from heat.

2. Stir together granulated sugar, water and corn syrup in small saucepan. Cook over medium heat, stirring constantly, until sugar is dissolved. Cook, without stirring, until mixture reaches 250°F on candy thermometer or until a small amount of syrup, when dropped into very cold water, forms a firm ball which does not flatten when removed from water. (Bulb of candy thermometer should not rest on bottom of saucepan.) Remove from heat; stir into chocolate mixture. Add vanilla, coconut and nuts; stir until well blended.

3. Refrigerate about 30 minutes or until firm enough to handle. Shape into 1-inch balls; roll in powdered sugar. Store tightly covered in cool, dry place.

About 4 dozen candies

NOTE: For best results, do not double this recipe.

PREP TIME: 25 minutes **COOK TIME:** 20 minutes **CHILL TIME:** 30 minutes

HERSHEY'S BUCKEYES

- **¾ cup (1½ sticks) butter or margarine, softened**
- **1⅓ cups REESE'S Crunchy Peanut Butter**
- **3 cups powdered sugar**
- **2 cups (12-ounce package) HERSHEY'S Semi-Sweet Chocolate Chips**
- **1 tablespoon shortening (do not use butter, margarine or oil)**

1. Beat butter and peanut butter in large bowl until blended. Gradually add powdered sugar, beating until well blended. Cover; refrigerate until firm enough to shape, about 30 minutes.

2. Shape into 1-inch balls. Cover; refrigerate until firm, about 1 hour.

3. Place chocolate chips and shortening in medium microwave-safe bowl. Microwave at HIGH (100%) 1½ minutes; stir. If necessary, microwave at HIGH an additional 15 seconds at a time, stirring after each heating, just until chips are melted when stirred.

4. Dip each ball into chocolate mixture, coating ¾ of ball. Place on wax paper, uncoated side up. Let stand until chocolate hardens. Store, covered, in refrigerator. *About 5 dozen candies*

PREP TIME: 30 minutes **CHILL TIME:** 1½ hours **COOK TIME:** 1½ minutes
COOL TIME: 1 hour

QUICK HOLIDAY RASPBERRY FUDGE

3⅓ cups (two 10-ounce packages) HERSHEY'S Raspberry Chips or 3⅓ cups HERSHEY'S Semi-Sweet Chocolate Chips
1 can (14 ounces) sweetened condensed milk (not evaporated milk)
1½ teaspoons vanilla extract or raspberry-flavored liqueur

1. Line 8-inch square pan with foil, extending foil over edges of pan.

2. Place raspberry chips and sweetened condensed milk in medium microwave-safe bowl. Microwave at HIGH (100%) 1 minute; stir. If necessary, microwave an additional 30 seconds at a time, stirring after each heating, just until chips are melted and mixture is smooth when stirred; stir in vanilla. Spread evenly into prepared pan.

3. Cover; refrigerate 2 hours or until firm. Remove from pan; place on cutting board. Peel off foil; cut into squares. Store loosely covered at room temperature. *About 4 dozen pieces or 2 pounds*

NOTE: For best results, do not double this recipe.

PREP TIME: 5 minutes **COOK TIME:** 1 minute **CHILL TIME:** 2 hours

CHOCOLATEY MOCHA CREME

- **1 package (6-serving size, about 5 ounces) chocolate cook & serve pudding and pie filling mix***
- **2 tablespoons powdered instant espresso**
- **3 cups skim milk**
- **2 cups (12-ounce package) HERSHEY'S Reduced Fat Semi-Sweet Baking Chips**
- **½ cup frozen light non-dairy whipped topping, thawed**
- **HERSHEY'S Cocoa**

**Do not use instant pudding mix.*

1. Stir pudding mix and instant espresso into milk in medium saucepan. Cook over medium heat, stirring constantly, until mixture comes to full boil; remove from heat. Add chips; stir until chips are melted and mixture is smooth. Spoon into small dessert dishes.

2. Press plastic wrap directly onto surface. Serve slightly warm or chilled. Garnish each with 1 tablespoon whipped topping. Dust with cocoa. *8 servings*

PREP TIME: 20 minutes **CHILL TIME:** 3 hours

NUTRITIONAL INFORMATION PER SERVING: ½ Cup
290 Calories (60 Calories from Fat), 7 g Total Fat* (11% Daily Value), 6 g Saturated Fat* (30% Daily Value), 0 mg Cholesterol (0% Daily Value), 120 mg Sodium (5% Daily Value), 51 g Total Carbohydrate (17% Daily Value), 3 g Dietary Fiber (12% Daily Value), 41 g Sugars, 6 g Protein, 2% Daily Value Vitamin A, 0% Daily Value Vitamin C, 120 mg Calcium (10% Daily Value) 6% Daily Value Iron

**Fat content adjusted for reduced availability of fat from Salatrim.*

Chocolatey Mocha Creme

SUNNY COCOA DROP COOKIES

½ cup (1 stick) 60% vegetable oil spread
⅔ cup granulated sugar
⅔ cup lowfat sour cream
1 egg white
1 teaspoon vanilla extract
¼ teaspoon freshly grated orange peel
1¾ cups all-purpose flour
3 tablespoons HERSHEY'S Cocoa
1 teaspoon baking soda
½ teaspoon baking powder
¼ teaspoon ground cinnamon
COCOA GLAZE (recipe follows)

1. Heat oven to 350°F. Spray cookie sheet with vegetable cooking spray.

2. Beat vegetable oil spread and granulated sugar in large bowl on medium speed of electric mixer until light and fluffy. Add sour cream, egg white, vanilla and orange peel; beat until well blended. Stir together flour, cocoa, baking soda, baking powder and cinnamon; gradually add to sugar mixture, beating until blended. Drop dough by rounded teaspoons onto prepared cookie sheet.

3. Bake 10 to 12 minutes or until set. Remove from cookie sheet to wire rack. Cool completely. Prepare COCOA GLAZE; drizzle over tops of cookies. Store, covered, at room temperature. *4 dozen cookies*

Cocoa Glaze

1 tablespoon 60% vegetable oil spread
2 tablespoons water
1 tablespoon HERSHEY'S Cocoa
½ cup powdered sugar
½ teaspoon vanilla extract

Melt vegetable oil spread in small saucepan over low heat. Stir in water and cocoa. Cook, stirring constantly, until thick. Do not boil. Remove from heat; gradually add powdered sugar and vanilla, beating with spoon or whisk to drizzling consistency. *About ⅓ cup glaze*

PREP TIME: 30 minutes **BAKE TIME:** 10 minutes

Nutritional Information Per Serving: 2 Cookies
100 Calories (35 Calories from Fat), 4 g Total Fat (6% Daily Value), 1 g Saturated Fat (5% Daily Value), <5 mg Cholesterol (1% Daily Value), 125 mg Sodium (5% Daily Value), 16 g Total Carbohydrate (5% Daily Value), <1 g Dietary Fiber (2% Daily Value), 9 g Sugars, 1 g Protein, 4% Daily Value Vitamin A, 0% Daily Value Vitamin C, 0% Daily Value Calcium, 2% Daily Value Iron

REDUCED FAT CHOCOLATEY SAUCE

- **2 cups (12-ounce package) HERSHEY'S Reduced Fat Semi-Sweet Baking Chips**
- **1 cup lowfat evaporated milk**
- **⅓ cup sugar**
- **1½ teaspoons vanilla extract**
- **Frozen yogurt or ice cream**

1. Place chips and evaporated milk in medium microwave-safe bowl. Microwave at HIGH (100%) 4 to 5 minutes, stirring after each minute of heating, until chips are melted and smooth.

2. Add sugar and vanilla; beat with whisk until well blended. Cool slightly. Serve over frozen yogurt or ice cream. Cover; refrigerate leftover sauce.

About 2 cups sauce

Note: To reheat sauce, place in small microwave-safe bowl. Microwave at HIGH 1 to 1½ minutes or until desired temperature

Prep Time: 3 minutes **Cook Time:** 4 minutes **Cool Time:** 10 minutes

Nutritional Information Per Serving: 2 Tablespoons
90 Calories (25 Calories from Fat), 2.5 g Total Fat* (4% Daily Value), 2 g Saturated Fat* (20% Daily Value), 0 mg Cholesterol (0% Daily Value), 0 mg Sodium (0% Daily Value), 15 g Total Carbohydrate (5% Daily Value), <1 g Dietary Fiber (4% Daily Value), 13 g Sugars, 2 g Protein, 0% Daily Value Vitamin A, 0% Daily Value Vitamin C, 25 mg Calcium (2% Daily Value), 6% Daily Value Iron

**Fat content adjusted for reduced availability of fat from Salatrim.*

CRUNCHY–TOPPED COFFEE CAKE WITH CHOCOLATEY CHIPS

1⅓ cups all-purpose flour
½ cup packed light brown sugar
¼ cup granulated sugar
½ teaspoon baking soda
¼ teaspoon baking powder
⅓ cup 60% vegetable oil spread, softened
½ cup buttermilk or sour milk*
¼ cup frozen egg substitute, thawed
1 cup HERSHEY'S Reduced Fat Semi-Sweet Baking Chips, divided
2 tablespoons finely chopped walnuts
Frozen light non-dairy whipped topping, thawed (optional)
Sliced strawberries (optional)

**To sour milk: Use 1½ teaspoons white vinegar plus milk to equal ½ cup.*

1. Heat oven to 350°F. Spray 9-inch round baking pan with vegetable cooking spray.

2. Stir together flour, brown sugar, granulated sugar, baking soda and baking powder in large bowl. Cut in spread until crumbly; reserve ½ cup mixture for topping. Stir together buttermilk and egg substitute; add to remaining crumb mixture, stirring until well blended. Spread batter into prepared pan. Sprinkle ¾ cup chips on top. Stir together reserved crumbs, remaining ¼ cup chips and walnuts; sprinkle on top.

3. Bake 25 to 30 minutes or until wooden pick inserted near center comes out clean. Cool in pan on wire rack. Cut into wedges; serve with dollop of whipped topping and sliced strawberries, if desired. *8 servings*

PREP TIME: 20 minutes **BAKE TIME:** 25 minutes **COOL TIME:** 1½ hours

NUTRITIONAL INFORMATION PER SERVING: 1 Piece
320 Calories (90 Calories from Fat), 10 g Total Fat* (15% Daily Value), 4 g Saturated Fat* (20% Daily Value), 0 mg Cholesterol (0% Daily Value), 170 mg Sodium (8% Daily Value), 52 g Total Carbohydrate (17% Daily Value), 2 g Dietary Fiber (8% Daily Value), 33 g Sugars, 5 g Protein, 10% Daily Value Vitamin A, 0% Daily Value Vitamin C, 50 mg Calcium (4% Daily Value) 10% Daily Value Iron

**Fat content adjusted for reduced availability of fat from Salatrim.*

Crunchy-Topped Coffee Cake with Chocolatey Chips

ELEGANT CHOCOLATE ANGEL TORTE

- 1/3 cup HERSHEY'S Cocoa
- 1 package (about 15 ounces) "two-step" angel food cake mix
- 2 envelopes (1.3 ounces each) dry whipped topping mix
- 1 cup cold skim milk
- 1 teaspoon vanilla extract
- 1 cup strawberry purée*
- Strawberries

**Mash 2 cups sliced fresh strawberries (or frozen berries, thawed) in blender or food processor. Cover; blend until smooth. Purée should measure 1 cup.*

1. Move oven rack to lowest position. Sift cocoa over contents of cake flour packet; stir to blend. Proceed with mixing cake as directed on package. Bake and cool as directed for 10-inch tube pan. Carefully run knife along side of pan to loosen cake; remove from pan. Using serrated knife, slice cake horizontally into four layers.

2. Prepare whipped topping mix as directed on package, using 1 cup milk and 1 teaspoon vanilla. Blend in strawberry purée. Place bottom cake layer on serving plate; spread with 1/4 of topping. Set next cake layer on top; spread with 1/4 of topping. Continue layering cake and topping. Garnish with strawberries. Refrigerate until ready to serve. Slice cake with sharp serrated knife, cutting with gentle sawing motion. Cover; refrigerate leftover cake.

About 16 servings

Prep Time: 30 minutes **Bake Time:** 45 minutes **Cool Time:** 2 hours

Nutritional Information Per Serving: 1 Piece
150 Calories (20 Calories from Fat), 2 g Total Fat (3% Daily Value), 2 g Saturated Fat (10% Daily Value), 0 mg Cholesterol (0% Daily Value), 210 mg Sodium (9% Daily Value), 28 g Total Carbohydrate (9% Daily Value), 1 g Dietary Fiber (4% Daily Value), 22 g Sugars, 4 g Protein, 0% Daily Value Vitamin A, 20% Daily Value Vitamin C, 50 mg Calcium (4% Daily Value), 2% Daily Value Iron

Elegant Chocolate Angel Torte

HERSHEY'S 50% REDUCED FAT CHOCOLATEY CHIP COOKIES

2¼ cups all-purpose flour
1 teaspoon baking soda
½ teaspoon salt
½ cup (1 stick) 60% vegetable oil spread
¾ cup granulated sugar
¾ cup packed light brown sugar
1 teaspoon vanilla extract
2 eggs
2 cups (12-ounce package) HERSHEY'S Reduced Fat Semi-Sweet Baking Chips

1. Heat oven to 375°F. Stir together flour, baking soda and salt in medium bowl.

2. Beat spread, granulated sugar, brown sugar and vanilla in large bowl with electric mixer until creamy. Add eggs; beat well. Gradually add flour mixture, beating well. Stir in chips. Drop by rounded teaspoons onto ungreased cookie sheet.

3. Bake 8 to 10 minutes or until lightly browned. Cool slightly; remove from cookie sheet to wire rack. *5 dozen cookies*

NOTE: To make softer, chewier cookies, add 1 or 2 tablespoons unsweetened applesauce to egg mixture.

PAN RECIPE: Spray 15½×10½×1-inch jelly-roll pan with vegetable cooking spray; spread batter into pan. Bake at 375°F 18 to 20 minutes or until lightly browned. Cool completely; cut into bars. *About 60 bars*

CHOCOLATE CHOCOLATEY CHIP COOKIES: Add ⅓ cup HERSHEY'S Cocoa to flour mixture; follow directions above for mixing and baking.

PREP TIME: 25 minutes **BAKE TIME:** 8 minutes

NUTRITIONAL INFORMATION PER SERVING: 1 Cookie
70 Calories (20 Calories from Fat), 2 g Total Fat* (3% Daily Value), 1 g Saturated Fat* (5% Daily Value), 5 mg Cholesterol (2% Daily Value), 60 mg Sodium (3% Daily Value), 13 g Total Carbohydrate (4% Daily Value), <1 g Dietary Fiber (3% Daily Value), 9 g Sugars, 1 g Protein, 0% Daily Value Vitamin A, 0% Daily Value Vitamin C, 0% Daily Value Calcium, 0% Daily Value Iron

**Fat content adjusted for reduced availability of fat from Salatrim. 2 g of fat per serving vs. 4.5 g in regular HERSHEY'S CLASSIC CHOCOLATE CHIP COOKIE.*

QUICK CHOCOLATE CUPCAKES

1½ cups all-purpose flour
¾ cup sugar
¼ cup HERSHEY'S Cocoa
1 teaspoon baking soda
½ teaspoon salt
1 cup water
¼ cup vegetable oil
1 tablespoon white vinegar
1 teaspoon vanilla extract
Powdered sugar (optional)

1. Heat oven to 375°F. Line muffin cups (2½ inches in diameter) with paper bake cups.

2. Stir together flour, sugar, cocoa, baking soda and salt in medium bowl. Add water, oil, vinegar and vanilla; beat with whisk just until batter is smooth and ingredients are well blended. Fill muffin cups ⅔ full with batter.

3. Bake 16 to 18 minutes or until wooden pick inserted in center comes out clean. Remove from pan to wire rack. Cool completely. Sift with powdered sugar, if desired. *16 cupcakes*

PREP TIME: 10 minutes **BAKE TIME:** 16 minutes **COOL TIME:** 1 hour

NUTRITIONAL INFORMATION PER SERVING: 1 Cupcake
110 Calories (30 Calories from Fat), 3.5 g Total Fat (5% Daily Value), 0.5 g Saturated Fat (3% Daily Value), 0 mg Cholesterol (0% Daily Value), 150 mg Sodium (6% Daily Value), 19 g Total Carbohydrate (6% Daily Value), <1 g Dietary Fiber (3% Daily Value), 10 g Sugars, 1 g Protein, 0% Daily Value Vitamin A, 0% Daily Value Vitamin C, 0% Daily Value Calcium, 4% Daily Value Iron

HERSHEY'S 50% REDUCED FAT CHOCOLATE SWIRLED CHEESEPIE

- **1 carton (8 ounces) lowfat vanilla yogurt**
- **½ cup graham cracker crumbs**
- **1 package (8 ounces) Neufchâtel cheese (⅓ less fat), softened**
- **½ cup sugar**
- **¾ teaspoon vanilla extract**
- **2 eggs**
- **1 cup HERSHEY'S Reduced Fat Semi-Sweet Baking Chips**
- **⅓ cup HERSHEY'S Syrup (do not use Lite Syrup)**

1. Line rust-proof colander with cheesecloth or large coffee filter; place colander over bowl. Spoon yogurt into prepared colander; drain 1 to 2 hours. Remove yogurt from cheesecloth; discard liquid.

2. Heat oven to 350°F. Lightly spray 9-inch pie plate with vegetable cooking spray. Sprinkle graham cracker crumbs on bottom of plate.

3. Beat Neufchâtel cheese, sugar and vanilla on medium speed of electric mixer until well blended. Add yogurt; beat well. Add eggs; beat well. Place chips and syrup in small microwave-safe bowl. Microwave at HIGH (100%) 45 seconds; stir until chips are melted. Gradually add ¾ cup cheese mixture, stirring until well blended. Alternately spoon vanilla and chocolate mixtures into prepared pan (chocolate will be thicker). Using knife, swirl for marbled effect.

4. Bake 30 to 35 minutes or until center is almost set. Cool. Refrigerate about 4 hours before serving. *8 to 10 servings*

Prep Time: 2¼ hours **Bake Time:** 30 minutes **Cool Time:** 1 hour
Chill Time: 4 hours

Nutritional Information Per Serving: 1 Piece

260 Calories (90 Calories from Fat), 10 g Total Fat* (15% Daily Value), 6 g Saturated Fat* (30% Daily Value), 60 mg Cholesterol (20% Daily Value), 160 mg Sodium (7% Daily Value), 37 g Total Carbohydrate (12% Daily Value), 1 g Dietary Fiber (4% Daily Value), 31 g Sugars, 6 g Protein, 6% Daily Value Vitamin A, 0% Daily Value Vitamin C, 6% Daily Value Calcium, 4% Daily Value Iron

**Fat content adjusted for reduced availability of fat from Salatrim. 10 g of fat per serving vs. 22 g in regular CHOCOLATE SWIRLED CHEESEPIE.*

Hershey's 50% Reduced Fat Chocolate Swirled Cheesepie

EASY CHOCOLATE LOVER'S CHEESEPIE

- **3 packages (8 ounces each) cream cheese, softened**
- **¾ cup sugar**
- **3 eggs**
- **1 teaspoon vanilla extract**
- **2 cups (12-ounce package) HERSHEY'S MINICHIPS Semi-Sweet Chocolate, divided**
- **1 extra serving-size packaged graham cracker crumb crust (9 ounces)**
- **2 tablespoons whipping cream**

1. Heat oven to 450°F. Beat cream cheese and sugar with electric mixer in large bowl until well blended. Add eggs and vanilla; beat well. Stir in 1⅔ cups small chocolate chips; pour into crust.

2. Bake 10 minutes. Without opening oven door, reduce temperature to 250°F; continue baking 30 minutes or just until set.

3. Remove from oven to wire rack. Cool completely. Cover; refrigerate until thoroughly chilled.

4. Place remaining ⅓ cup chips and whipping cream in small microwave-safe bowl.

5. Microwave at HIGH (100%) 20 to 30 seconds or just until chips are melted and mixture is smooth when stirred. Cool slightly; spread over top of cheesepie. Refrigerate 15 minutes or until topping is set. Cover; refrigerate leftover cheesepie. *10 servings*

Prep Time: 15 minutes **Bake Time:** 40 minutes
Cool Time: 1 hour **Chill Time:** 4 hours

Easy Chocolate Lover's Cheesepie

EASY CHOCOLATE CREAM–FILLED TORTE

1 frozen pound cake (10¾ ounces), thawed
½ cup powdered sugar
¼ cup HERSHEY'S Cocoa
1 cup (½ pint) cold whipping cream
1 teaspoon vanilla extract
CHOCOLATE GLAZE (recipe follows)
Sliced almonds (optional)

1. Cut cake horizontally to make 4 layers. Stir together sugar and cocoa in medium bowl. Add whipping cream and vanilla; beat until stiff.

2. Place bottom cake layer on serving platter. Spread ⅓ of the whipped cream mixture on cake layer. Place next cake layer on top of whipped cream; continue layering whipped cream mixture and cake until all have been used.

3. Prepare CHOCOLATE GLAZE; spoon over top of cake, allowing to drizzle down sides. Garnish with almonds, if desired. Refrigerate until ready to serve. Cover; refrigerate leftover torte. *8 to 10 servings*

Chocolate Glaze

2 tablespoons butter or margarine
2 tablespoons HERSHEY'S Cocoa
2 tablespoons water
1 cup powdered sugar
¼ to ½ teaspoon almond extract

1. Melt butter in small saucepan over low heat. Add cocoa and water. Cook, stirring constantly, until smooth and slightly thickened. Do not boil.

2. Remove from heat. Gradually add powdered sugar and almond extract, beating with whisk until smooth. *About ½ cup glaze*

PREP TIME: 20 minutes **CHILL TIME:** 30 minutes

Easy Chocolate Cream-Filled Torte

COCOA CAPPUCCINO MOUSSE

- **1 can (14 ounces) sweetened condensed milk (not evaporated milk)**
- **⅓ cup HERSHEY'S Cocoa**
- **3 tablespoons butter or margarine**
- **2 teaspoons powdered instant coffee or espresso, dissolved in 2 teaspoons hot water**
- **2 cups (1 pint) cold whipping cream**

1. Combine sweetened condensed milk, cocoa, butter and coffee in medium saucepan. Cook over low heat, stirring constantly, until butter melts and mixture is smooth. Remove from heat; cool.

2. Beat whipping cream in large bowl until stiff. Gradually fold chocolate mixture into whipped cream. Spoon into dessert dishes. Refrigerate until set, about 2 hours. Garnish as desired. *8 servings*

PREP TIME: 15 minutes **COOK TIME:** 10 minutes **CHILL TIME:** 2 hours

CHOCOLATE CHEESEPIE

- **1 package (8 ounces) cream cheese, softened**
- **1 package (3 ounces) cream cheese, softened**
- **¾ cup sugar**
- **1 teaspoon vanilla extract**
- **¼ cup HERSHEY'S Cocoa**
- **2 eggs**
- **½ cup whipping cream**
- **1 packaged graham cracker crumb crust (6 ounces)**
- **Cherry pie or peach pie filling or sliced fresh fruit**

1. Heat oven to 350°F. Beat cream cheese, sugar and vanilla in large bowl until well blended.

2. Add cocoa; beat until well blended; scraping sides of bowl and beaters frequently. Add eggs; beat well. Stir in whipping cream. Pour into crust.

3. Bake 35 to 40 minutes. (Center will be soft but will set upon cooling.) Cool to room temperature. Cover; refrigerate several hours or overnight. Serve with pie filling. Cover; refrigerate leftover pie. *6 to 8 servings*

PREP TIME: 10 minutes **BAKE TIME:** 35 minutes **CHILL TIME:** 4 to 6 hours

Cocoa Cappuccino Mousse

CHOCOLATE CHERRY CREAM–FILLED LOG

4 eggs, separated
½ cup granulated sugar
1 teaspoon vanilla extract
⅓ cup granulated sugar
⅓ cup HERSHEY'S Cocoa
½ cup all-purpose flour
¼ teaspoon baking powder
¼ teaspoon baking soda
⅛ teaspoon salt
⅓ cup water
Powdered sugar
1 can (21 ounces) cherry pie filling, divided
1½ cups whipped topping
CHOCOLATE GLAZE (recipe page 228)

1. Heat oven to 375°F. Line 15½×10½×1/2-inch jelly-roll pan with foil; generously grease foil.

2. Beat egg whites in large bowl until foamy; gradually add ½ cup granulated sugar, beating until stiff peaks form.

3. Beat egg yolks and vanilla in small bowl on high speed for about 3 minutes. Gradually add ⅓ cup granulated sugar; continue beating 2 minutes. Combine cocoa, flour, baking powder, baking soda and salt; add to egg yolk mixture alternately with water on low speed, beating just until batter is smooth.

4. Fold chocolate mixture gradually into egg whites; spread evenly in prepared pan.

5. Bake 12 to 15 minutes or until top springs back when touched lightly in center. Immediately loosen cake from edges of pan; invert on towel sprinkled with powdered sugar. Carefully remove foil. Immediately roll cake in towel starting from narrow end; place on wire rack to cool.

6. Combine 1 cup pie filling and whipped topping, mix well. Unroll cake; remove towel. Spread with filling; reroll cake.

7. Prepare CHOCOLATE GLAZE; drizzle over top, allowing to run down sides of cake. Refrigerate several hours. Just before serving, spoon ½ cup pie filling over cake. Serve with remaining pie filling. *10 to 12 servings*

(continued on page 234)

Chocolate Cherry Cream-Filled Log

(Chocolate Cherry Cream-Filled Log, continued)

Chocolate Glaze

2 tablespoons butter or margarine
2 tablespoons HERSHEY'S Cocoa
2 tablespoons water
1 cup powdered sugar
½ teaspoon vanilla extract

1. Melt butter in small saucepan over low heat. Add cocoa and water. Cook, stirring constantly, until smooth and slightly thickened. Do not boil.

2. Remove from heat; cool slightly. Gradually blend in sugar and vanilla.

PREP TIME: 30 minutes **BAKE TIME:** 12 minutes **COOL TIME:** 1 hour
CHILL TIME: 3 hours

HOT FUDGE PUDDING CAKE

1¼ cups granulated sugar, divided
1 cup all-purpose flour
7 tablespoons HERSHEY'S Cocoa, divided
2 teaspoons baking powder
¼ teaspoon salt
½ cup milk
⅓ cup butter or margarine, melted
1½ teaspoons vanilla extract
½ cup packed light brown sugar
1¼ cups hot water
Whipped topping

1. Heat oven to 350°F. Stir together ¾ cup granulated sugar, flour, 3 tablespoons cocoa, baking powder and salt. Stir in milk, butter and vanilla; beat until smooth.

2. Pour batter into ungreased 9-inch square baking pan. Stir together remaining ½ cup granulated sugar, brown sugar and remaining 4 tablespoons cocoa; sprinkle mixture evenly over batter. Pour hot water over top. Do not stir.

3. Bake 35 to 40 minutes or until center is almost set. Let stand 15 minutes; spoon into dessert dishes, spooning sauce from bottom of pan over top. Garnish with whipped topping. *About 8 servings*

PREP TIME: 10 minutes **BAKE TIME:** 35 minutes **COOL TIME:** 15 minutes

BITTERSWEET TRUFFLE TOFFEE MOUSSE PIE

1¾ cups (10-ounce package) SKOR English Toffee Bits or 1¾ cups HEATH Bits 'O Brickle, divided
1 tablespoon water
1 package (8 ounces) cream cheese, softened
4 bars (1 ounce each) HERSHEY'S Bittersweet Baking Chocolate, divided
1 cup (½ pint) cold whipping cream, divided
1 baked (9 inch) pie crust, cooled
½ teaspoon shortening (do not use butter, margarine or oil)

1. Combine 1 cup toffee bits and water in small saucepan. Cook over medium heat, stirring constantly, until toffee is melted. Gradually beat toffee mixture into cream cheese in medium bowl. Refrigerate 20 minutes.

2. Place 3 ounces chocolate and 3 tablespoons whipping cream in small microwave-safe bowl. Microwave at HIGH (100%) 1 minute; stir. If necessary, microwave an additional 15 seconds or until chocolate is melted and mixture is smooth when stirred. Spread chocolate mixture onto bottom of baked crust; refrigerate.

3. Beat remaining whipping cream in small bowl until stiff; gradually stir into toffee mixture, mixing thoroughly. Gently stir in ½ cup bits. Spread over chocolate layer. Cover; refrigerate until well chilled, about 3 hours.

4. Shortly before serving, place remaining 1 bar of chocolate and shortening in small microwave bowl. Microwave at HIGH 1 minute or until chocolate is melted and smooth when stirred; drizzle over top of pie. Garnish with remaining ¼ cup toffee bits. Refrigerate until drizzle is set. Cover; refrigerate leftover pie. *6 to 8 servings*

PREP TIME: 30 minutes **COOK TIME:** 12 minutes **CHILL TIME:** 3½ hours

ITALIAN RICOTTA TORTE

8 eggs, separated
1½ cups sugar, divided
1½ cups ground blanched almonds
⅔ cup all-purpose flour
⅔ cup HERSHEY'S Cocoa
1 teaspoon baking soda
½ teaspoon salt
½ cup water
2 teaspoons vanilla extract
½ teaspoon almond extract
RICOTTA CHERRY FILLING (recipe page 238)
COCOA WHIPPED CREAM (recipe page 238)
Candied cherries or sliced almonds (optional)

1. Heat oven to 375°F. Grease bottoms of two 9-inch round baking pans; line with wax paper. Grease wax paper lining leaving sides of pans ungreased.

2. Beat egg yolks in large bowl on medium speed of electric mixer 3 minutes. Gradually add 1 cup sugar, beating another 2 minutes. Stir together almonds, flour, cocoa, baking soda and salt; add alternately with water to egg yolk mixture, beating on low speed just until blended. Stir in vanilla and almond extract.

3. Beat egg whites in large bowl until foamy. Gradually add remaining ½ cup sugar, beating until stiff peaks form. Carefully fold chocolate mixture into beaten egg whites. Spread batter evenly into prepared pans.

4. Bake 20 to 22 minutes or until top springs back when touched lightly. Cool 10 minutes; remove from pans to wire racks. Cool completely. With long serrated knife, cut each layer in half horizontally to make 4 thin layers. Refrigerate layers while preparing filling and whipped cream.

5. Place one cake layer on serving plate; spread with ⅓ (about 1⅓ cups) RICOTTA CHERRY FILLING. Top with another cake layer. Repeat with remaining filling and cake layers. Frost sides and top of torte with COCOA WHIPPED CREAM. Garnish with candied cherries or almonds, if desired. Refrigerate at least 4 hours. Cover; refrigerate leftover torte.

8 to 10 servings

(continued on page 238)

Italian Ricotta Torte

(Italian Ricotta Torte, continued)

Ricotta Cherry Filling

1 cup (½ pint) cold whipping cream
1¾ cups (15 ounces) ricotta cheese
⅓ cup powdered sugar
½ cup chopped candied cherries
½ teaspoon almond extract

1. Beat whipping cream in small bowl until stiff. Beat ricotta cheese and powdered sugar in large bowl until smooth.

2. Fold whipped cream into cheese mixture just until blended. Stir in candied cherries and almond extract. *About 4 cups filling*

COCOA WHIPPED CREAM: Stir together ⅔ cup powdered sugar and ⅓ cup HERSHEY'S Cocoa in large bowl. Add 2 cups (1 pint) cold whipping cream and 2 teaspoons vanilla extract; beat just until stiff. (Do not overbeat.) *About 4 cups*

PREP TIME: 40 minutes **BAKE TIME:** 20 minutes **COOL TIME:** 1 hour
CHILL TIME: 4 hours

MINI CHOCOLATE PIES

1 package (4-serving size) chocolate cook & serve pudding and pie filling mix*
1 cup HERSHEY'S MINICHIPS Semi-Sweet Chocolate
1 package (4 ounces) single serve graham cracker crusts (6 crusts)
Whipped topping
Additional MINICHIPS Semi-Sweet Chocolate

**Do not use instant pudding mix.*

1. Prepare pudding and pie filling mix as directed on package; remove from heat. Immediately add 1 cup small chocolate chips; stir until melted. Cool 5 minutes, stirring occasionally.

2. Pour filling into crusts; press plastic wrap directly onto surface. Refrigerate several hours or until firm. Garnish with whipped topping and small chocolate chips. *6 servings*

PREP TIME: 5 minutes **COOK TIME:** 10 minutes **COOL TIME:** 5 minutes
CHILL TIME: 2 hours

Mini Chocolate Pies

SKOR BITS SAUCE

1¾ cups (10-ounce package) SKOR English Toffee Bits or 1¾ cups HEATH Bits 'O Brickle
½ cup whipping cream
2 tablespoons light corn syrup
2 tablespoons butter
Vanilla ice cream

1. Stir together toffee bits, whipping cream and corn syrup in small saucepan.

2. Cook over medium heat, stirring constantly, until mixture comes to a boil. Remove from heat.

3. Add butter; stir until melted. Cool. Serve over ice cream.

About 1⅔ cups sauce

PREP TIME: 2 minutes **COOK TIME:** 10 minutes **COOL TIME:** 20 minutes

REESE'S PEANUT BUTTER 'N' CHOCOLATE PIE

1⅓ cups HERSHEY'S MINI KISSES Chocolate, divided
2 tablespoons milk
1 packaged crumb crust (6 ounces)
1 package (8 ounces) Neufchâtel cheese (⅓ less fat), softened
¾ cup sugar
1 cup REESE'S Creamy or Crunchy Peanut Butter
3½ cups (8 ounces) frozen non-dairy whipped topping, thawed

1. Place ⅔ cup MINI KISSES and milk in small microwave-safe bowl . Microwave at HIGH (100%) 30 to 45 seconds or just until melted and smooth when stirred; spread evenly onto bottom of crust. Cover; refrigerate.

2. Beat Neufchâtel cheese in medium bowl until smooth; gradually beat in sugar. Stir in peanut butter and whipped topping until blended; spoon evenly into crust over chocolate mixture. Cover; refrigerate until set, at least 4 hours.

3. Place remaining ⅔ cup chocolate pieces around edge of filling just before serving. Serve cold; cover and refrigerate leftover pie.

8 servings

PREP TIME: 20 minutes **COOK TIME:** 30 seconds **CHILL TIME:** 4 hours

My Favorites

My Favorite Recipes

Favorite recipe: ______________________________

Favorite recipe from: ______________________________

Ingredients: ______________________________

____

____

____

____

____

Method: ______________________________

____

____

____

____

____

____

____

____

____

____

____

____

My Favorite Recipes

Favorite recipe: ______________________________

Favorite recipe from: ______________________________

Ingredients: ______________________________

____

____

____

____

____

Method: ______________________________

____

____

____

____

____

____

____

____

____

____

____

____

My Favorite Recipes

Favorite recipe: ____________________

Favorite recipe from: ____________________

Ingredients: ____________________

Method: ____________________

My Favorite Recipes

Favorite recipe: ______________________________

Favorite recipe from: ______________________________

Ingredients: ______________________________

Method: ______________________________

My Favorite Recipes

Favorite recipe: ______________________________

Favorite recipe from: ______________________________

Ingredients: ______________________________

____

____

____

____

____

Method: ______________________________

____

____

____

____

____

____

____

____

____

____

____

____

My Favorite Recipes

Favorite recipe: ____________________

Favorite recipe from: ____________________

Ingredients: ____________________

____

____

____

____

____

Method: ____________________

____

____

____

____

____

____

____

____

____

____

____

____

My Favorite Recipes

Favorite recipe: ______________________________

Favorite recipe from: ______________________________

Ingredients: ______________________________

Method: ______________________________

My Favorite Recipes

Favorite recipe:

Favorite recipe from:

Ingredients:

Method:

My Favorite Recipes

Favorite recipe: ______________________

Favorite recipe from: ______________________

Ingredients: ______________________

Method: ______________________

My Favorite Recipes

Favorite recipe: ______________________________

Favorite recipe from: ______________________________

Ingredients: ______________________________

____

____

____

____

____

Method: ______________________________

____

____

____

____

____

____

____

____

____

____

____

____

My Favorite Recipes

Favorite recipe: ______________________________

Favorite recipe from: ______________________________

Ingredients: ______________________________

Method: ______________________________

My Favorite Recipes

Favorite recipe: ______________________________

Favorite recipe from: ______________________________

Ingredients: ______________________________

____

____

____

____

____

Method: ______________________________

____

____

____

____

____

____

____

____

____

____

____

____

My Favorite Recipes

Favorite recipe: ______________________________

Favorite recipe from: ______________________________

Ingredients: ______________________________

____

____

____

____

____

Method: ______________________________

____

____

____

____

____

____

____

____

____

____

____

____

My Favorite Recipes

Favorite recipe: ____________________

Favorite recipe from: ____________________

Ingredients: ____________________

____

____

____

____

____

Method: ____________________

____

____

____

____

____

____

____

____

____

____

____

____

My Favorite Recipes

Favorite recipe: ______________________________

Favorite recipe from: ______________________________

Ingredients: ______________________________

____

____

____

____

____

Method: ______________________________

____

____

____

____

____

____

____

____

____

____

____

____

My Favorite Recipes

Favorite recipe: ____________________

Favorite recipe from: ____________________

Ingredients: ____________________

Method: ____________________

My Favorite Recipes

Favorite recipe: ______________________________

Favorite recipe from: ______________________________

Ingredients: ______________________________

____

____

____

____

____

Method: ______________________________

____

____

____

____

____

____

____

____

____

____

____

____

My Favorite Recipes

Favorite recipe: ______________________________

Favorite recipe from: ______________________________

Ingredients: ______________________________

Method: ______________________________

My Favorite Recipes

Favorite recipe: ____________________

Favorite recipe from: ____________________

Ingredients: ____________________

Method: ____________________

My Favorite Recipes

Favorite recipe: ____________________

Favorite recipe from: ____________________

Ingredients: ____________________

____

____

____

____

____

Method: ____________________

____

____

____

____

____

____

____

____

____

____

____

____

My Favorite Dinner Party

Date: ______________________

Occasion: ______________________

Guests: ______________________

Menu: ______________________

My Favorite Dinner Party

Date: ______________________________

Occasion: ______________________________

____

Guests: ______________________________

____

____

____

____

Menu: ______________________________

____

____

____

____

____

____

____

____

____

____

____

____

My Favorite Dinner Party

Date: ______________________________

Occasion: ______________________________

____

Guests: ______________________________

____

____

____

____

Menu: ______________________________

____

____

____

____

____

____

____

____

____

____

____

____

My Favorite Dinner Party

Date: ____

Occasion: ____

____

Guests: ____

____

____

____

____

Menu: ____

____

____

____

____

____

____

____

____

____

____

____

____

My Favorite Brunch

Date: ______________________________

Occasion: ______________________________

____

Guests: ______________________________

____

____

____

____

Menu: ______________________________

____

____

____

____

____

____

____

____

____

____

____

____

My Favorite Brunch

Date: ______________________________

Occasion: ______________________________

____

Guests: ______________________________

____

____

____

____

Menu: ______________________________

____

____

____

____

____

____

____

____

____

____

____

____

My Favorite Brunch

Date:

Occasion:

Guests:

Menu:

My Favorite Brunch

Date: ____________________

Occasion: ____________________

Guests: ____________________

Menu: ____________________

My Favorite Food Gifts

Friend: ______________________________

Date: ______________________________

Food Gift: ______________________________

____

____

____

Friend: ______________________________

Date: ______________________________

Food Gift: ______________________________

____

____

____

Friend: ______________________________

Date: ______________________________

Food Gift: ______________________________

____

____

____

My Favorite Food Gifts

Friend: ____________________

Date: ____________________

Food Gift: ____________________

____

____

____

Friend: ____________________

Date: ____________________

Food Gift: ____________________

____

____

____

Friend: ____________________

Date: ____________________

Food Gift: ____________________

____

____

____

My Favorite Friends

Friend: ______________________________

Favorite foods: ______________________________

____

Don't serve: ______________________________

____

____

Friend: ______________________________

Favorite foods: ______________________________

____

Don't serve: ______________________________

____

____

Friend: ______________________________

Favorite foods: ______________________________

____

Don't serve: ______________________________

____

____

My Favorite Friends

Friend: ____________________

Favorite foods: ____________________

____

Don't serve: ____________________

____

____

Friend: ____________________

Favorite foods: ____________________

____

Don't serve: ____________________

____

____

Friend: ____________________

Favorite foods: ____________________

____

Don't serve: ____________________

____

____

Hints, Tips & Index

Baking Basics

• Read the entire recipe before you begin to be sure you have all the necessary ingredients and utensils.

• Remove butter, margarine and cream cheese from the refrigerator to soften, if necessary.

• Adjust oven racks and preheat the oven. Check oven temperature with an oven thermometer to make sure the temperature is accurate.

• Toast and chop nuts and melt butter and chocolate before preparing batter or dough.

• Always use the pan size suggested in the recipe. Prepare pans as directed.

• Choose cookie sheets that fit in your oven with at least 1 inch on all sides between the edge of the sheet and the oven wall.

• Grease cookie sheets only when the recipe recommends it; otherwise, the cookies may spread too much.

• Measure the ingredients accurately and assemble them in the order they are listed in the recipe.

• When baking more than one sheet of cookies at a time, it's best to rotate them for even baking. Halfway through the baking time, rotate the cookie sheets from front to back as well as from the top rack to the bottom rack.

• Always check for doneness at the minimum baking time given in the recipe.

Melting Chocolate

There are several methods for melting chocolate. They all begin with utensils that are completely dry. Moisture, whether from utensils or an accidental drop of water, causes chocolate to "seize," which means it becomes stiff and grainy. If this happens, try adding a ½ teaspoon of shortening (not butter or margarine, which contain water) for each ounce of chocolate and stir until smooth. Also avoid high heat because chocolate scorches easily and once scorched cannot be used. Follow one of these three methods for successful melting.

Double Boiler:
This is the safest method because it prevents scorching. Place the chocolate in the top of a double boiler or in a heatproof bowl over hot, not boiling, water; stir until smooth. (Make sure that the water remains just below a simmer and is 1 inch below the bottom of the top pan.) Be careful that no steam or water gets into the chocolate.

Direct Heat:
Place the chocolate in a heavy saucepan and melt over very low heat, stirring constantly. Remove the chocolate from the heat as soon as it is melted. Be sure to watch the chocolate carefully because it scorches easily when using this method.

Microwave Oven:
Place an unwrapped 1-ounce square or 1 cup of chocolate chips in a small microwavable bowl. Microwave on HIGH 1 to 1½ minutes, stirring after 1 minute. Be sure to stir microwaved chocolate since it may retain its original shape even when melted. It will taste burnt if microwaved after it has melted. Chocolate can also be melted in a small heavy resealable plastic food storage bag, turning the bag over after microwaving 1 minute. When the chocolate is melted, knead the bag until chocolate is smooth. Cut off a tiny corner of the bag and gently squeeze the bag to drizzle the chocolate.

Decorating

Great-looking baked goods go a long way toward making a special dessert or bake sale successful. A few extra minutes spent on decorating can make all the difference. Try any of the following ideas to jazz up your cakes, cookies and pies

Chocolate Drizzle
Melted chocolate or white chocolate provides an easy finish for many baked goods. Simply drizzle melted chocolate with a spoon or fork over baked goods or dip half of each cookie in melted chocolate. The contrast of a white chocolate drizzle on a brown chocolate cookie is sure to draw attention.

Chocolate Leaves
Chocolate leaves provide a sensational garnish for a layer cake. Add 1 teaspoon shortening (not butter or margarine) for every 2 ounces of chocolate and melt. Brush the underside of clean, dry, nontoxic leaves, such as lemon, rose or camellia, with melted chocolate until the leaves are thickly and evenly coated. Wipe off any excess chocolate from the front of the leaves. Place leaves, chocolate side up, on waxed paper; let them stand in a cool, dry place until firm. (Do not refrigerate.) When chocolate is firm, carefully grasp the stems and peel leaves away from chocolate. Use immediately or chill until ready to use.

Chocolate Curls
This elegant and impressive garnish is the perfect topping for layer cakes. Add 1 teaspoon shortening (not butter or margarine) for every 2 ounces of chocolate and melt. Cool melted chocolate slightly; pour chocolate onto the back of a jelly-roll pan. Quickly spread it into a thin layer with a flat metal spatula. Let stand in a cool, dry place until the chocolate is firm. (Do not refrigerate.) When chocolate is just firm, hold an offset metal spatula at a 45° angle and scrape chocolate into curls. Use a small skewer or wooden toothpick to transfer curls to waxed paper; store curls in a cool, dry place or use immediately.

Decorating

Powdered Sugar Glaze
A simple glaze drizzled or spread on quick breads, coffee cakes or other baked goods is an attractive and easy topping. Combine 1 cup sifted powdered sugar and 5 teaspoons milk in a small bowl. Add ½ teaspoon vanilla extract or other flavoring, if desired. Stir until smooth. If the glaze is too thin, stir in additional powdered sugar; if the consistency is too thick, add additional milk, ½ teaspoon at a time.

Toasting Nuts
Chopped nuts make a great topping on frosted treats. Toasting nuts intensifies their flavor and fragrance. To toast nuts, spread them in a single layer on a cookie sheet. Bake in a preheated 325°F oven for 8 to 10 minutes or until golden, stirring occasionally to ensure even toasting. The nuts will darken and become crisper as they cool. To toast a small amount of nuts, place them in a dry skillet over low heat. Stir constantly for 2 to 4 minutes or until the nuts darken slightly and become fragrant. Always cool nuts before using.

Toasting Coconut
Coconut sprinkled on frosted cakes, brownies and cookies adds a distinctive appearance and flavor. To toast coconut, spread a thin layer of flaked coconut on a cookie sheet. Bake in a preheated 325°F oven for 7 to 10 minutes. Shake the pan or stir the coconut occasionally during baking to promote even browning and prevent burning.

Tinting Coconut
Tinted coconut is a festive finish for cupcakes. To tint coconut, simply dilute a few drops of liquid food coloring with ½ teaspoon milk or water in a small bowl. Add 1 to 1⅓ cups flaked coconut and toss with a fork until coconut is evenly tinted.

Storing and Freezing

Cookies & Bars

Unbaked cookie dough can be refrigerated for up to one week or frozen for up to six weeks. Rolls of dough (for slice-and-bake cookies) should be sealed tightly in plastic wrap; other doughs should be stored in airtight containers. For convenience, label plastic wrap or container with baking information.

Store soft and crisp cookies separately at room temperature to prevent changes in texture and flavor. Keep soft cookies in airtight containers. If they begin to dry out, add a piece of apple or a slice of bread to the container to help them retain moisture. Store crisp cookies in containers with loose-fitting lids to prevent moisture buildup. If the cookies become soggy, heat the undecorated ones in a 300°F oven for 3 to 5 minutes to restore crispness. Store cookies with sticky glazes, fragile decorations and icings in single layers between sheets of waxed paper.

As a rule, crisp cookies freeze better than soft, moist cookies. Rich, buttery bar cookies are an exception because they freeze extremely well. Freeze baked cookies in airtight containers or freezer bags for up to six months. Thaw cookies and brownies unwrapped at room temperature. Meringue-based cookies do not freeze well and chocolate-dipped cookies will discolor if frozen.

Cakes

Store one-layer frosted cakes in their baking pans, tightly covered. Store layered frosted cakes under a cake cover or under a large inverted bowl. Cakes with whipped cream frostings or cream fillings should be stored in the refrigerator. Unfrosted cakes can be frozen for up to four months if well-wrapped in plastic; thaw them, unwrapped, at room temperature.

Frosted cakes should be frozen unwrapped until the frosting hardens, and then wrapped, sealed and frozen for up to two months. To thaw, remove the wrapping and thaw at room temperature or in the refrigerator. Cakes with fruit or custard fillings do not freeze well because they become soggy when thawed.

Storing and Freezing

Pies
Unbaked pie dough can be frozen for later use. Simply flatten the dough into disks and stack them in a freezer bag with waxed paper separating the layers. Freeze prepared pastry shells in pie pans with waxed paper between the shells. Disks of pie dough must be thawed before using them whereas pastry shells should be baked frozen.

Meringue-topped pies are best when served the day they are made; leftovers should be refrigerated. Custard or cream pies should be refrigerated immediately after cooling. Fruit pies should be covered and stored at room temperature overnight; refrigerate them for longer storage.

To freeze unbaked fruit pies, do not cut steam vents in the top crust. Cover them with inverted paper plates for extra protection and package in freezer bags or plastic wrap. To bake, do not thaw. Cut slits in the top crust and allow an additional 15 to 20 minutes of baking time. Baked fruit pies can be frozen after they are completely cooled. To serve, let the pie thaw at room temperature for two hours, then heat until warm. Pies with cream or custard fillings and meringue toppings do not freeze well.

Breads & Muffins
Quick breads should be wrapped well in plastic wrap and stored at room temperature to stay fresh up to one week. Or, they may be frozen for up to three months wrapped in heavy-duty foil. Muffins should be stored in a sealed plastic food storage bag up to three days. Or, they may be frozen for up to one month wrapped in heavy-duty foil.

How Much of This = That?

Almonds, blanched, slivered	4 ounces = 1 cup
Butter	2 cups = 1 pound or 4 sticks 1 cup = ½ pound or 2 sticks ½ cup = 1 stick or 8 tablespoons ¼ cup = ½ stick or 4 tablespoons
Chocolate	1 (6-ounce) package chocolate chips = 1 cup chips or 6 (1-ounce) squares semisweet chocolate
Cocoa, unsweetened	1 (8-ounce) can = 2 cups
Coconut, flaked	3½ ounces = 1⅓ cups
Cream cheese	1 (3-ounce) package = 6 tablespoons 1 (8-ounce) package = 1 cup
Flour	
white or all-purpose	1 pound = 3½ to 4 cups
whole-wheat	1 pound = 3¾ to 4 cups
Honey, liquid	16 ounces = 1⅓ cups
Milk	
Evaporated	1 (5-ounce) can = ⅔ cup 1 (12-ounce) can = 1⅔ cups
Sweetened, condensed	14-ounce can = 1¼ cups
Shortening	1 pound = 2½ cups
Sugar	
Granulated	1 pound = 2½ cups
Brown, packed	1 pound = 2¼ cups
Confectioners' or powdered	1 pound = 3¾ to 4 cups, unsifted

I Know I Don't Have

If you don't have:	Use:
1 teaspoon baking powder	½ teaspoon baking soda plus ¼ teaspoon cream of tartar
½ cup firmly packed brown sugar	½ cup sugar mixed with 2 tablespoons molasses
1 ounce (1 square) unsweetened baking chocolate	3 tablespoons unsweetened cocoa plus 1 tablespoon shortening
3 ounces (3 squares) semisweet baking chocolate	3 ounces (½ cup) semisweet chocolate morsels
1 cup sweetened whipped cream	4½ ounces thawed frozen whipped topping
1 cup heavy cream (for baking, not whipping)	¾ cup whole milk plus ¼ cup butter
1 cup cake flour	1 cup minus 2 tablespoons all-purpose flour
1 cup honey	1¼ cups granulated sugar plus ¼ cup water
1 package active dry yeast	1 cake compressed yeast

General Substitutions

If you don't have:	Use:
1 cup buttermilk	1 tablespoon lemon juice or vinegar plus milk to equal 1 cup (stir; let stand 5 minutes)
1 tablespoon cornstarch	2 tablespoons all-purpose flour or 2 teaspoons arrowroot
1 whole egg	2 egg yolks plus 1 teaspoon cold water
1 teaspoon vinegar	2 teaspoons lemon juice
1 cup whole milk	1 cup skim milk plus 2 tablespoons melted butter
1 cup sour cream	1 cup plain yogurt

Common Weights and Measures

Dash = less than ⅛ teaspoon

½ tablespoon = 1½ teaspoons

1 tablespoon = 3 teaspoons

2 tablespoons =⅛ cup

¼ cup = 4 tablespoons

⅓ cup = 5 tablespoons plus 1 teaspoon

½ cup = 8 tablespoons

¾ cup = 12 tablespoons

1 cup = 16 tablespoons

½ pint = 1 cup or 8 fluid ounces

1 pint = 2 cups or 16 fluid ounces

1 quart = 4 cups or 2 pints or 32 fluid ounces

1 gallon = 16 cups or 4 quarts

1 pound = 16 ounces

Metric Conversion Chart

VOLUME MEASUREMENTS (dry)

1/8 teaspoon = 0.5 mL
1/4 teaspoon = 1 mL
1/2 teaspoon = 2 mL
3/4 teaspoon = 4 mL
1 teaspoon = 5 mL
1 tablespoon = 15 mL
2 tablespoons = 30 mL
1/4 cup = 60 mL
1/3 cup = 75 mL
1/2 cup = 125 mL
2/3 cup = 150 mL
3/4 cup = 175 mL
1 cup = 250 mL
2 cups = 1 pint = 500 mL
3 cups = 750 mL
4 cups = 1 quart = 1 L

VOLUME MEASUREMENTS (fluid)

1 fluid ounce (2 tablespoons) = 30 mL
4 fluid ounces (1/2 cup) = 125 mL
8 fluid ounces (1 cup) = 250 mL
12 fluid ounces (1 1/2 cups) = 375 mL
16 fluid ounces (2 cups) = 500 mL

WEIGHTS (mass)

1/2 ounce = 15 g
1 ounce = 30 g
3 ounces = 90 g
4 ounces = 120 g
8 ounces = 225 g
10 ounces = 285 g
12 ounces = 360 g
16 ounces = 1 pound = 450 g

DIMENSIONS

1/16 inch = 2 mm
1/8 inch = 3 mm
1/4 inch = 6 mm
1/2 inch = 1.5 cm
3/4 inch = 2 cm
1 inch = 2.5 cm

OVEN TEMPERATURES

250°F = 120°C
275°F = 140°C
300°F = 150°C
325°F = 160°C
350°F = 180°C
375°F = 190°C
400°F = 200°C
425°F = 220°C
450°F = 230°C

BAKING PAN SIZES

Utensil	Size in Inches/Quarts	Metric Volume	Size in Centimeters
Baking or Cake Pan (square or rectangular)	8×8×2	2 L	20×20×5
	9×9×2	2.5 L	23×23×5
	12×8×2	3 L	30×20×5
	13×9×2	3.5 L	33×23×5
Loaf Pan	8×4×3	1.5 L	20×10×7
	9×5×3	2 L	23×13×7
Round Layer Cake Pan	8×1½	1.2 L	20×4
	9×1½	1.5 L	23×4
Pie Plate	8×1¼	750 mL	20×3
	9×1¼	1 L	23×3
Baking Dish or Casserole	1 quart	1 L	—
	1½ quart	1.5 L	—
	2 quart	2 L	—

Acknowledgments

The publisher would like to thank the companies and organizations listed below for the use of their recipes and photographs in this publication.

Best Foods Division, CPC International Inc.

Blue Diamond Growers

Bob Evans®

California Prune Board

California Tree Fruit Agreement

Cherry Marketing Institute, Inc.

Diamond Walnut Growers, Inc.

Dole Food Company, Inc.

Duncan Hines® brand is a registered trademark of Aurora Foods Inc.

Filippo Berio Olive Oil

Hershey Foods Corporation

Kraft Foods, Inc.

Land O' Lakes, Inc.

M & M/MARS

Nabisco, Inc.

National Honey Board

Nestlé USA

The Quaker® Kitchens

Southeast United Dairy Industry Association, Inc.

Sunkist Growers

Washington Apple Commission

Wisconsin Milk Marketing Board

Index

Index

Index

Index

Index